AFOLABI SAMUEL COKER

THE DIVINE SETTLER

Unless otherwise indicated, all scripture
references are from The King James
Version of the Holy Bible.

ISBN : 978-978-949-989-2

Published by:
Bolaan Ventures
42, Association Avenue, Ilupeju, Lagos, Nigeria.
Telephones: + 234 803 337 4095, +234 802 318 9259
E-mail: afocoker@yahoo.com
Blog: pastorcoker.blogspot.com
Twitter: @pastor_coker
Facebook: Facebook.com/afolabiandadetutucoker

Printed by:
Olu Arogbodo Printing Works
Tel: 0803 398 2304, 0802 069 7445
E-mail: jamesolowo@gmail.com

DEDICATION

This book is dedicated to all those who desire positive changes in life; and those who believe in the power of THE DIVINE SETTLER.

May you be totally transformed in Jesus name.

Proverbs 23:18

ACKNOWLEDGMENTS

I bless the name of THE DIVINE SETTLER, the Lord most high for inspiring this book. May Your name alone be glorified forever. I acknowledge Your grace upon my life, family and works. Without You I cannot do anything. Thank You Father.

My thanks also go to the faithful partners of SETTLE, ME O LORD! Outreach, and all members of the working team for their financial and prayer supports. God bless you all.

I must not fail to acknowledge Pastors Olayemi and Jadesola Onigbode and the United Kingdom working team for their continual support. May the face of the Lord continually shine upon you.

A big God bless you and thank you to Pastor Akintunde Olusoji Dawodu and minister (DR) Nkiruka David for their contributions toward the editing of the manuscript, and all others who have contributed in one way or the other to make this book a reality.

And to my son Olorunfemi Coker, thank you for your technical assistance. May God increase you greatly.

Last but not the least, the publisher; my virtuous wife, Rev (Dr.) Adetutu Omolola Coker for painstakingly and sacrificially toiling day and night for weeks to ensure that this dream becomes a reality in print. I appreciate you, my love and complete help mate. I am forever grateful for your roles in my destiny.

Thank you all!

INTRODUCTION

THE DIVINE SETTLER

1 Peter 5:10

But may the God of all grace, who called us to His eternal glory by Christ Jesus, after you have suffered a while, perfect, establish, strengthen, and settle you. (NKJV)

Luke 4:18-19

"The Spirit of the LORD is upon Me, Because He has anointed Me To preach the gospel to the poor; He has sent Me to heal the brokenhearted, To proclaim liberty to the captives And recovery of sight to the blind, To set at liberty those who are oppressed; To proclaim the acceptable year of the LORD." (NKJV)

Isaiah 61:1-3

"The Spirit of the Lord GOD is upon Me, Because the LORD has anointed Me To preach good tidings to the poor; He has sent Me to heal the brokenhearted, To proclaim liberty to the captives, And the opening of the prison to those who are bound; To proclaim the acceptable year of the LORD, And the day of vengeance of our God; To comfort all who mourn, To console those who mourn in Zion, To give them beauty for ashes, The oil of joy for mourning, The garment of praise for the spirit of heaviness; That they may be called trees of righteousness, The planting of the LORD, that He may be glorified." (NKJV)

The predetermined will of the Lord is to progressively perfect, establish, strengthen and SETTLE His people. Although many are the afflictions of men, His will is to make the end to be better than the beginning.

As a result, He died for you to live. He suffered for you to live in pleasure, He went through for you to come through, He became poor so that you can be rich. He was wounded for our transgression, bruised for our iniquities and by His stripes you were healed.

We have Him as our great, most compassionate High Priest who is touched by our infirmities. He has gone through these challenges before we manifest them.

He encourages us to come boldly to His throne of Grace, so to as settle all controversies and issues of life.

"Seeing then that we have a great High Priest who has passed through the heavens, Jesus the Son of God, let us hold fast our confession. For we do not have a High Priest who cannot sympathize with our weaknesses, but was in all points tempted as we are, yet without sin. Let us therefore come boldly to the throne of grace, that we may obtain mercy and find grace to help in time of need". (Hebrews 4:14-16 NKJV)

As you go through this book passionately with faith in your heart, you will see the glory of God made manifest in your life in the name of Jesus.

I believe that the DIVINE SETTLER who is the author and finisher of our Faith will settle the issues of your life for real.

Read through, meditate on the principles of the dynamics of Jesus Christ's assignments in this book ,receive the Impartation ,and pray the prayer topics aggressively with faith in your heart. You will encounter the eternal magnificent splendor of God for your SETTLEMENT.

The Spirit of the Lord will rest upon you.

The anointing of The Lord will be expressive in your life to perfect, establish , strengthen and SETTLE all that God has for you here on earth without delay.

Divine comfort, joy, beauty, praise, restoration, favour be yours as His tree of righteousness so that
God will always be fully glorified in your life.

Remember that God's thought towards you is of good, better life, good welfare, assured future, fulfilled destiny and not of evil. *(Jeremiah 29:11).*

As you give it what it takes in practicing the keys of DIVINE SETTLEMENT, His grace will see you through for the better.

TABLE OF CONTENTS

THE DIVINE SETTLER

Chapter One

JESUS CHRIST,
THE DIVINE SETTLER

Jesus Christ divinely settles those who truly believe in Him. He is not only the King of kings, but also the Lord of Lords. ***Revelation 19:16.***

A lord is one who affects superiority and authority over another.

He is the One who says in ***Ezekiel 36:11:***
"And I will multiply upon you man and beast; and they shall increase and bring fruit: and I will settle you after your old estates, and will do better unto you than at your beginnings: and ye shall know that I am the Lord". ***KJV***

Let us see what other versions of the Bible say about this for more clarification:
NLT says; *"I will make you more prosperous..."*
AMP says; *"I will do better for you..."*
NCV says; *"I will make you better off..."*
CEB says; *"I will do you more good than ever before..."*
GWT says; *"I will make you better than ever before..."*

Jesus is the same yesterday, today and forever. What He said in time past, he is saying today.

He makes things happen. He can reverse the irreversible.

He makes a way where there is no way. If He made a way through the Red Sea, He will make a way for you through the difficulties you are passing through.

Except Jesus makes things happen, nobody else can.

HE IS:
* The exact image of God. *Hebrews 1:3, John 14:9; 2 Corinthians 4:4; Colossians 1:15*
* The first and the last, the Alpha and the Omega. *Revelation 22:13;Revelation1:17; 2:8; 21:6*
* The Word of God. *John 1:1,14;Malachi 3:1; 1John 1:1;Revelation 19:13*
* The last Adam. *1Corinthians 15:45;Romans 5:14*
* The bright Morning Star. *Revelation 22:16;2Peter 1:19*
* The rising Sun. *Malachi 4:2;Luke 1:78*
* The Living One. *Revelation 1:18;John 5:26;11:25*
* The Amen. *Revelation 3:14;2Corinthians 1:20*
* The true Light. *John 1:3-9;3:19-21;Isaiah 9:2;Luke 2:32;John 8:12;12:46*
* The Righteous One. *Acts 3:14; Jeremiah 23:6;33:15-16; Acts 7:52;22:14*
* The Lion of Judah. *Revelation 5:5*
* The King of the Jews.*Matthew2:1-2; 27:37;John 8:58.*
* The Bread of life. *John 6:35*
* The Light of the world. *John 8:12;9:5*
* The Gate. *John 10:7-10*
* The Good Shepherd. *John 10:11-14*
* The Resurrection and the Life. *John 11:25*
* The Way, The Truth and Life .*John 14:6*
* The True Vine. *John 15:1-5*
* The seed of Abraham.*Galatians3:16; Genesis 12:7;*

13:15; 24:7

* The Root and Offspring of David. *Revelation 22:16*
* The faithful Witness. *Revelation 1:5;3:14;Isaiah 55:4; John 18:37.*
* Immanuel. *Matthew 1:23;Isaiah 7:14;8:8*
* The Capstone. *Matthew 21:42 ; Mark 12:10 ; Luke 20:17; Psalm 118:22; Acts 4:11; Ephesians 2:20-21; 1 Peter 2:6-7*
* The Rock. *1 Corinthians 10:4; Isaiah 8:14; 28:16; Romans 9:32-33; 1Peter 2:8*
* The Bridegroom. *John 3:29*
* The Firstborn among many brothers. *Romans 8:29*
* The First fruit. *1Corinthians 15:23.*
* The Firstborn from the dead. *Revelation1:5*
* The Heir of all things.*Hebrews1:2*
* Lord. *Acts 2:25; Matthew 7:21; Luke 6:46; John 6:68; Romans 10:13; 1 Corinthians3:5; Colossians 3:23; 2 Peter1:11*
* The Head of the church. *Ephesians 1:22-23; 4:15; 5:23; Colossians 2:19*
* The Chief Shepherd.*1Peter 5:4; Matthew 2:6; Micah 5:2; John 10:11; 1 Peter 2:25;Hebrews 13:20*
* Prince. *Acts 5:31*
* Rabbi. *John 1:38,49; 20:16*
* Jesus: the Lord saves. *Matthew 1:21*
* Man of sorrows. *Isaiah 53:3*
* The Passover Lamb. *1 Corinthians 5:7*
* A Horn of salvation. *Luke 1:69*
* The Consolation of Israel. *Luke 1:68; 2:25,38*
* The Deliverer and Redeemer. *Romans 11:26; Isaiah 59:20*
* The Author and Perfecter of salvation. *Hebrews 2:10; 5:9; 12:2*
* The Mediator. *1 Timothy 2:5*

* The High Priest. *Hebrews 3:1; 2:17; 6:20*
* The Son of Man. *Luke 5:24; 19:10, Matthew 11:19; John 3:13; 6:53; Acts 7:56; Revelation 1:13*

HE IS:

* Jesus, the Christ.
* Christ, Son of David.
* Christ, Son of God.
* Christ, Son of Man.
* Christ, the Lord.
* Immanuel.

HE IS:

* The Unchangeable Changer.
* The Custodian of all things.
* The Stone of Israel.
* The Shepherd of our soul.
* The Governor General.
* The Rock of Ages.
* The Bright morning Star.
* The Daystar.
* The Lord of Life.
* The Lord of glory.
* The Lamb.
* The True and ultimate Sacrifice.
* The Last Adam.
* The Life Giving Spirit.
* The Lily of the Valley.
* The Immortal, Invisible and the Only wise God.
* The same yesterday, today and forever.
* The miracle worker.
* The Blesser.
* The Divine Intervenor.

* The Unchangeable Changer.
* The Immovable Mover.
* The Unstoppable Stopper.
* Our Righteousness, Wisdom, Sanctification and Redeemer.
* Never elected nor voted to power.
* There was nothing that was made, that was made without Him.
* He is the God of all possibilities.
* The God of unlimited possibilities.
* Our Eternal Rock of ages.
* There is no impossibility with Him.
* The God of unlimited possibilities.

"For with God nothing will be impossible" (Luke 1:37)
Jesus said to him, *"If you can believe, all things are possible to him who believes." (Mark 9:23 NKJV)*

"But Jesus looked at them and said, "With men it is impossible, but not with God; for with God all things are possible." (Mark 10:27 NKJV)

THE SPIRIT OF THE SETTLER

The Holy Ghost is the Spirit of The settler.
HE IS:
* The Spirit of God. *Genesis 1:2; 41:38; 1 Samuel 10:10; 19:20,23; Romans 8:9; 1 Corinthians 6:11; 2 Corinthians 3:3; Ephesians 4:30; Philippians 3:3*
* The Spirit of the Lord. *Judges 3:10; 6:34; 11:29; 13:25; 14:6,19; 15:14; 1 Samuel 10:6; 16:13; 2 Samuel 23:2*
* My Spirit. *Genesis 6:3; Isaiah 30:1; 59:21; Joel 2:28-29; Haggai 2:5; Zechariah 4:6; 6:8; Matthew 12:18*
* His Spirit. *Isaiah 34:16; Isaiah 63:10-11; Zechariah 7:12;*

Romans 8:11.

* Your Spirit.*Nehemiah9:20,30; Psalm 51:11;143:10*
* The Spirit of your Father. *Matthew 10:20*
* The promised Holy Spirit. *Acts 2:33; Galatians 4:6; Acts 16:7; Romans 8:9; Philippians 1:19; 1 Peter 1:11*
* The Spirit of truth. *John 16:13; 14:17; 15:26; 1 John 4:6*
* The Spirit of holiness. *Romans 1:4*
* The Spirit of life. *Romans 8:2*
* The Spirit of glory. *1 Peter 4:14*
* The eternal Spirit. *Hebrew 9:14*
* The Counsellor. *John 14:26; 15:26*
* The Spirit of wisdom and understanding. *Isaiah 11:2; Deuteronomy 34:9; Ephesians 1:17*
* The Spirit of grace and supplication. *Zechariah 12:10*.
* The Spirit of sonship. *Romans 8:15*
* The Spirit of judgment and fire. *Isaiah 4:4*
* The breath of God.
* He is the Spirit of Grace.
* The Spirit of Life and The Life giving Spirit.
* The Spirit of God.
* The Holy Spirit.
* The Spirit of truth. Comforter, Helper, Advocate, Intercessor, Strengthener and Standby.
* The Paraclete, a friend that sticks closer to one than a brother.
* The Administrator of the Godhead body.

The Spirit of the Settler will do wonders in you ,with you and through you.

"How God anointed Jesus of Nazareth with the Holy Spirit and with power, who went about doing good and healing all who were oppressed by the devil, for God was with Him" (Acts

10:38 NKJV)

"Then Jesus returned in the power of the Spirit to Galilee, and news of Him went out through all the surrounding region." (Luke 4:14)

"Men of Israel, hear these words: Jesus of Nazareth, a Man attested by God to you by miracles, wonders, and signs which God did through Him in your midst, as you yourselves also know" (Acts 2:22)

"Therefore they stayed there a long time, speaking boldly in the Lord, who was bearing witness to the word of His grace, granting signs and wonders to be done by their hands". (Acts14:3).

No matter the duration of your trouble, problem, suffering, pain, fear, insecurity, uncertainty, affliction, shame and anxiety, the Lord will set you free by neutralizing every device of the enemy against you.

I don't know the nature of your problem. It might be spiritual, psychological, financial, mental, emotional, medical, physical, marital, biological, academical, professional or otherwise. It doesn't matter how the problem came, or for how long it has been with you, I am happy to announce to you that The Ancient of days is interested in your case. He is the God of all possibilities. He is more than able. He will fight for you and give you victory. Trust in Him and obey Him. Have faith in Him and His word and you will soon testify of His goodness.

Turn your battles over to Him, and you will take delivery of your victory in Jesus name.

His word says in **Psalm 34:19** that;
"Many are the afflictions of the righteous: but the Lord delivered him out of them all"

Moreover He said, *"I am the God of your father the God of Abraham, the God of Isaac, and the God of Jacob."* And Moses hid his face, for he was afraid to look upon God. And the LORD said;
"I have surely seen the oppression of My people who are in Egypt, and have heard their cry because of their taskmasters, for I know their sorrows. So I have come down to deliver them out of the hand of the Egyptians, and to bring them up from that land to a good and large land, to a land flowing with milk and honey, to the place of the Canaanites and the Hittites and the Amorites and the Perizzites and the Hivites and the Jebusites. Now therefore, behold, the cry of the children of Israel has come to Me, and I have also seen the oppression with which the Egyptians oppress them. " (Exodus 3:6-9 NKJV)

1 Peter 5:10 says *"after you have suffered for awhile..."*

God will divinely perfect, establish, strengthen and settle you. He will show up for you. He will frustrate every move of the enemy to derail you in Jesus name. Good doors will open unto you on their own accord.

WHO WILL HE SETTLE ?
HE IS SENT TO:
1. HEAL THE BROKEN HEARTED

* The Divine Settler is sent to the broken hearted.
* Are you forsaken, battered and bruised?
* Have your friends and loved ones let you down?
* Have trusted ones betrayed your trust?

* May be you are grieving the loss of a loved one...
* Perhaps what gave you joy is now giving you sorrow.
* Are you a person of sorrowful spirit as Hannah?

The Divine Settler will settle you exceeding abundantly if you can believe. Like Hannah, He will wipe away your tears and grant your heart's desires.

"But Hannah answered and said, "No, my lord, I am a woman of sorrowful spirit. I have drunk neither wine nor intoxicating drink, but have poured out my soul before the LORD. "Do not consider your maidservant a wicked woman, for out of the abundance of my complaint and grief I have spoken until now." Then Eli answered and said, "Go in peace, and the God of Israel grant your petition which you have asked of Him." (I Samuel 1:15-17 NKJV)

Proverbs 15:13b says; *"but by sorrow of the heart the spirit is broken."*
Is your spirit broken? Are you sorrowful? Are you in distress, are you in debt, or tied up in a web of difficulties? Hear what the word of God says;
"And everyone who was in distress, everyone who was in debt, and everyone who was discontented gathered to him. So he became captain over them. And there were about four hundred men with him. " (I Samuel 22:2 NKJV)

Are you in the strong hold of life challenges? David was in the same situation in *1 Samuel 22:4-5:*
"So he brought them before the king of Moab, and they dwelt with him all the time that David was in the stronghold. Now the prophet Gad said to David, "Do not stay in the stronghold; depart, and go to the land of Judah." So David departed and

went into the forest of Hereth. (I Samuel 22:4-5 NKJV)

The Lord who saw David through will see you through.

From henceforth you are departing into the land of Praise (Judah). You will no more abide in the strong hold.

You are triumphantly victorious because you are more than a conqueror. You are a mighty man and woman of valor. You are lifted and highly favored in the name of Jesus.

"For His anger is but for a moment, His favor is for life; Weeping may endure for a night, But joy comes in the morning." (Psalm 30:5 NKJV)

Are you going through godly or ungodly sorrow?

"For godly sorrow produces repentance leading to salvation, not to be regretted; but the sorrow of the world produces death." (II Corinthians 7:10 NKJV)

Whatever it may be, God will settle you in the name of Jesus. I decree over your life: No more sorrow in Jesus name. The Divine Settler Himself will satiate the weary soul and replenish every sorrowful soul in the name of Jesus.

"For I have satiated the weary soul, and I have replenished every sorrowful soul." (Jeremiah 31:25 NKJV)

In *1 Chronicles 4:9-10*, Jabez was settled from sorrow to honour. His life experienced a total turnaround. He became more honorable than his siblings and peers.

"Now Jabez was more honorable than his brothers, and his mother called his name Jabez, saying, "Because I bore him in pain." And Jabez called on the God of Israel saying, "Oh, that

You would bless me indeed, and enlarge my territory, that Your hand would be with me, and that You would keep me from evil, that I may not cause pain!" So God granted him what he requested. " (I Chronicles 4:9-10 NKJV)

"And the ransomed of the LORD shall return, And come to Zion with singing, With everlasting joy on their heads. They shall obtain joy and gladness, And sorrow and sighing shall flee away." (Isaiah 35:10 NKJV).

"And God will wipe away every tear from their eyes; there shall be no more death, nor sorrow, nor crying. There shall be no more pain, for the former things have passed away." (Revelation 21:4 NKJV).

* Therefore, I decree into your life, that from henceforth your story will be :
* From pain to profit.
* From shame to glory.
* From curses to blessings.
* From lack to abundance.
* From story to glory.
* Like Jabez, you will move from the state of hopelessness to hopefulness.
* No more sorrow, but pleasantness in Jesus name.
* No more pains, but gains in Jesus name.
* You will no more eat crumbs but will wine and dine with Kings and Nobles in the mighty name of Jesus.
* You will no more experience defeats, no more loss, no more death of good and profitable things in Jesus name.
* You are totally set free from sorrow!
* No more indebtedness, you will no more live from hand

to mouth. An end has come to whatever has been frustrating you before now. I decree a complete separation between you and frustration in Jesus name.

* You will no more fail. Failure will give way to success in your life in Jesus name because failure is now a thing of the past in your life.

* I decree enmity between you and whatever kills your joy. Joy killer shall no more locate you in Jesus name.
* No more depression in the name of Jesus.
* Behold joy cometh to you.

The Divine Settler has turned your mourning into dancing. Your ashes have given way to beauty. For you there shall no more be a dull moment in Jesus name. The word of God in Isaiah 61:3 shall be your testimony;

"To appoint unto them that mourn in Zion, to give unto them beauty for ashes, the oil of joy for mourning, the garment of praise for the spirit of heaviness; that they might be called trees of righteousness, the planting of the Lord, that he might be glorified. " (Isaiah 61:3 KJV)

The Divine Settler will give you a new and a better laughter. Concerning you and your household, it shall be gladness unlimited in Jesus name.

You shall sing new songs and dance new dances. New testimonies shall fill your mouth and there shall be no end to celebrations in your lives in Jesus name.

All these are possible by the name of the Settler, the name that is above all names, Jesus, at whose mention every knee must bow and every mouth confess. The name that delivers and saves.

The name of the Settler will work wonders in your life in Jesus name.

2. SET THE CAPTIVE FREE

"Many are the afflictions of the righteous, But the LORD delivers him out of them all." *(Psalm 34:19 NKJV)*

"The thief does not come except to steal, and to kill, and to destroy. I have come that they may have life, and that they may have it more abundantly." *(John 10:10 NKJV)*

"Stay with me; do not fear. For he who seeks my life seeks your life, but with me you shall be safe." *(I Samuel 22:23 NKJV)*

Jesus has come to proclaim liberty to the captive, and to give people personal freedom.

You will from henceforth walk in liberty.

Please learn to seek the divine Settler's precepts. Follow after Him and you will never go astray.

"And I will walk at liberty, For I seek Your precepts." *(Psalm 119:45 NKJV)*

He has come to set those in the prison of troubled waters, troubled rivers and troubled fire of life free. I have good news for you, if you have been held by demonic servitude, unseen barriers, limitations, confinement and oppression, the Divine Settler Himself has come to put an end to your oppression.

The word of God says in *Isaiah 41:10-14:*
"Fear not, for I am with you; Be not dismayed, for I am your God. I will strengthen you, Yes, I will help you, I will uphold

you with My righteous right hand.' "Behold, all those who were incensed against you Shall be ashamed and disgraced; They shall be as nothing, And those who strive with you shall perish. You shall seek them and not find them Those who contended with you. Those who war against you Shall be as nothing, As a nonexistent thing. For I, the LORD your God, will hold your right hand, Saying to you, 'Fear not, I will help you.' "Fear not, you worm Jacob, You men of Israel! I will help you," says the LORD And your Redeemer, the Holy One of Israel. "

Have you been imprisoned or enslaved, bruised, incapacitated spiritually, emotionally, mentally, maritally, biologically, career wise?

Have you been afflicted by forces that are contrary to the plan and purpose of God for your life? are you under the yoke of lack, retrogression, frustration, failure, retrogression, abject poverty, lack of results, fruitless efforts, sickness, disease, lack of favour, lack, barrenness, stagnation, dryness, poverty, dishonor, lack of change of status, no promotion, no spouse, no child or secondary infertility etc?

The Divine Settler Himself will change your situation for good. He is the unchanging Changer. He specializes in doing the unexpected and lifting the undeserving. Just in one night, he changed Joseph from a prisoner into a Prime Minister *(Genesis 41)*

Just look up to Him and you will be settled. Remain faithful to Him, walk before Him blameless and He will delight in you.

3. REMOVE BARRIERS

"Lift up your heads, O you gates! And be lifted up, you everlasting doors! And the King of glory shall come in. Who is this King of glory? The LORD strong and mighty, The LORD mighty in battle. Lift up your heads, O you gates! Lift up, you everlasting doors! And the King of glory shall come in. Who is this King of glory? The LORD of hosts, He is the King of glory." (Psalm24:7-10 NKJV)

Another name of the Divine Settler is The King of glory.

As nothing can stop the entrance of the King of glory into any place He wishes to go, nothing or nobody will be able to hinder your entrance into greatness in the mighty name of Jesus.

By virtue of reading this book, you are in for the greatest encounter you can ever imagine.

Every barrier to your promotion and breakthrough will give way in Jesus name.

Every limitation to your accomplishments will come to an end in Jesus name.

When God lifts, no one can bring down. When He promotes no one can demote. The Settler will cause every barrier that has kept you on the same spot for so long to be history very soon.

He is the unstoppable God. No wonder He says in *Isaiah 43:13:*
"Yea, before the day was I am he; and there is none that can deliver out of my hand: I will work, and who shall let it?"

Whatever obstacle the Divine Settler removes for you shall

be permanently removed.

When He decides to bless you, nothing can stop Him, not even your doubts.

Gates of limitations are lifted for your sake.

Gates of impossibilities are removed for you.

You will no more be constrained to a spot in the mighty name of Jesus.

Doors of greatness will open to you on their own accord.

Is it not written concerning you in *1 Corinthians 16:9: "For a great and effective door has opened to me, and there are many adversaries."*

The Lord will fight for you. You will see the end of your adversaries.

God will root out everything He has not planted in you.

"And even now the axe is laid to the root of all the trees. Therefore every tree which does not bear good fruit is cut down and thrown into the fire." (Luke 3:9 NKJV)

4. HEAL THE SICK

The Divine settler is also the great Physician who heals all our infirmities. Sickness can be described as the condition of being ill, or being affected with illness or disease. It is a general state of being unwell. Sickness comes in many forms.

Jesus has come to set things right in our lives. He is a need meeting God. He is the Most High God who can overrule any sickness or disease. He can also overrule death.

I therefore prophesy into your life-that sickness will not conquer you.

That illness will not see your end in Jesus name.

Whatever the devil has programmed for you is cancelled in Jesus name.

Perhaps you are already battling with death, probably your case has been written off and everyone is waiting for you to die, I decree into your life, that death is overruled now.

I command your ailing business to receive fresh life now. Your dying ministry will receive the life of God now in Jesus name!

That barren womb will receive life now!

When you are connected to the Divine Settler, death cannot have a hold on you, neither can sickness control your life.

The Divine Settler shall quicken every part of your body to life now. You will not die but live.

His body was broken by the stripes He received for you. *1Peter 2:24* says, we have been healed by the stripes.

Receive your liberty from every hold of sickness now in Jesus name.

I decree, be delivered, be set free, be healed, be cured in Jesus name. You will progress, advance, and be promoted. You will be repositioned, be restored, be well favored, be more honorable in Jesus name. I decree you will prosper and be lifted, you will be blessed and be fruitful. You will be graced and your situation will change for the better.

For the reader who desires to be married, your desire will

come to pass in the name of Jesus.

I command you to begin to walk in the liberty wherewith Christ has made you free in the name of Jesus.

"Stand fast therefore in the liberty by which Christ has made us free, and do not be entangled again with a yoke of bondage."(Galatians 5:1 NKJV)

So endeavor to look continually into the perfect law of liberty and be a doer of the word. Stay tuned to the word of God at all times and live by it.

"But be doers of the word, and not hearers only, deceiving yourselves. For if anyone is a hearer of the word and not a doer, he is like a man observing his natural face in a mirror; for he observes himself, goes away, and immediately forgets what kind of man he was. But he who looks into the perfect law of liberty and continues in it, and is not a forgetful hearer but a doer of the work, this one will be blessed in what he does." (James 1:22-25 NKJV)

Knowing fully that our light affliction is just for a moment and will not last forever, I decree that you will no more be taken captive to do the devil's will anymore , in the name of Jesus.

"and that they may come to their senses and escape the snare of the devil, having been taken captive by him to do his will. " (II Timothy 2:26 NKJV)

Surely , the Divine Settler will show up for you against the forces that might have held you captive in the name of Jesus.

"Awake, awake, Deborah! Awake, awake, sing a song! Arise,

Barak, and lead your captives away, O son of Abinoam! "Then the survivors came down, the people against the nobles; The LORD came down for me against the mighty. " (Judges 5:12-13 NKJV)

Therefore, whatever that is not of God that has held you bound be cast out now in the name of Jesus.

"casting down arguments and every high thing that exalts itself against the knowledge of God, bringing every thought into captivity to the obedience of Christ." (II Corinthians 10:5 NKJV).

5. CAUSE RECOVERY OF SIGHT TO THE BLIND

The Divine Settler recovers and restores whatever is good that the enemy has stolen. He restores destinies, hopes, dreams, and visions.

Have you lost so much that you feel that the end is imminent? You will recover all. Jesus has come to set free those that are covered, bound, or blind.

Every spiritual blindness, deafness and dumbness will be cured, in the name of Jesus.

I decree Perfect Soundness of mind, explosive illumination, revelation knowledge, wisdom, insight and good understanding in the name of Jesus.

You will operate in His power and dominion without ceasing in the name of Jesus.

"But at midnight Paul and Silas were praying and singing hymns to God, and the prisoners were listening to them. Suddenly there was a great earthquake, so that the foundations

of the prison were shaken; and immediately all the doors were opened and everyone's chains were loosed. " (Acts 16:25-26 NKJV)

I decree in the mighty name of Jesus:
* Your chains are be broken in Jesus name.
* Your fetters are loosed.
* Every gate of brass binding you are cut asunder, in Jesus name.
* No more spiritual blindness.
* No more spiritual deafness.
* No more spiritual dumbness.
* The prison doors are flung open, and you are released to fulfill your destiny, in Jesus name.
* The ancient doors are lifted.
* The heavens over you are opened.
* The rightful divinely ordained doors of God will open for you on their own accord.
* No more curse.
* No more delays in the name of Jesus.
* I decree the blessings of God that add no sorrow into your business and endeavors.
* You will enjoy divine rest over all your labour.
* God will divinely elevate you.
* He will divinely cover you with His favour, goodness and mercy.
* Supernatural rewards will be your portion.
* I decree divine speed in every of your godly journeys, in Jesus name.
* I decree divine shift into all your endeavors, divine settlements into your life, in the name of Jesus.
* I decree triumphant shout of victory and good success into your life in the name of Jesus.

* Your fame shall spread throughout the whole country for good.

Joshua 6:27 says:

"So the LORD was with Joshua, and his fame spread throughout all the country. "

* God will be with you.
* God will be for you.
* God will endorse the good works of your hand.
* God will divinely announce your good works.
* He will vindicate and establish you in the name of Jesus.
* The Lord, the Chief Commander of the heavenly hosts will avenge your cause according to *Psalm 94:1-2;*

"O LORD God, to whom vengeance belongs O God, to whom vengeance belongs, shine forth! Rise up, O Judge of the earth; Render punishment to the proud."

"Let God arise, Let His enemies be scattered; Let those also who hate Him flee before Him. As smoke is driven away, So drive them away; As wax melts before the fire, So let the wicked perish at the presence of God. But let the righteous be glad; Let them rejoice before God; Yes, let them rejoice exceedingly." (Psalm 68:1-3 NKJV)

"Oh, let the wickedness of the wicked come to an end, But establish the just; For the righteous God tests the hearts and minds. My defense is of God, Who saves the upright in heart. God is a just judge, And God is angry with the wicked every day."(Psalm 7:9-11 NKJV)

"God is jealous, and the LORD avenges; The LORD avenges and is furious. The LORD will take vengeance on His

adversaries, And He reserves wrath for His enemies; The LORD is slow to anger and great in power, And will not at all acquit the wicked. The LORD has His way In the whirlwind and in the storm, And the clouds are the dust of His feet. He rebukes the sea and makes it dry, And dries up all the rivers. Bashan and Carmel wither, And the flower of Lebanon wilts. The mountains quake before Him, The hills melt, And the earth heaves at His presence, Yes, the world and all who dwell in it. Who can stand before His indignation? And who can endure the fierceness of His anger? His fury is poured out like fire, And the rocks are thrown down by Him. The LORD is good, A stronghold in the day of trouble; And He knows those who trust in Him. But with an overflowing flood He will make an utter end of its place, And darkness will pursue His enemies. What do you conspire against the LORD? He will make an utter end of it. Affliction will not rise up a second time. For while tangled like thorns, And while drunken like drunkards, They shall be devoured like stubble fully dried.

From you comes forth one Who plots evil against the LORD, A wicked counselor. Thus says the LORD: "Though they are safe, and likewise many, Yet in this manner they will be cut down When he passes through. Though I have afflicted you, I will afflict you no more; For now I will break off his yoke from you, And burst your bonds apart." The LORD has given a command concerning you: "Your name shall be perpetuated no longer. Out of the house of your gods I will cut off the carved image and the molded image. I will dig your grave, For you are vile." Behold, on the mountains The feet of him who brings good tidings, Who proclaims peace! O Judah, keep your appointed feasts, Perform your vows. For the wicked one shall no more pass through you; He is utterly cut off." (Nahum 1:2-15 NKJV)

From henceforth, you will run like an Elijah.

I pray that God our Father and the Lord Jesus Christ will give you much more grace and peace.

Your speed to success will no more be hindered in the name of Jesus. It will no more be slow.

Backwardness and retrogression are no more your lot in Jesus name.

I pray that money will become like common stone to you, in the name of Jesus.

2 Chronicles 9:27-28 says;
"During his reign silver was as common in Jerusalem as stone, and cedar was as plentiful as ordinary sycomore in the foothills of Judah. Solomon imported horses from Musri and from every other country" (2 Chronicles 9:27-28 GNB)

God will do for you what He did for Ezra.

You will be favored beyond your contemporaries.

"By God's grace I have won the favour of the emperor, of his counsellors, and of all his powerful officials; the Lord my God has given me courage, and I have been able to persuade many of the heads of the clans of Israel to return with me." (Ezra 7:28 GNB)

He will also do for you greater than the accomplishments of Solomon.

"Solomon loved the Lord and followed the instructions of his father David, but he also slaughtered animals and offered them as sacrifices on various altars. On one occasion he went to Gibeon to offer sacrifices because that was where the most

famous altar was. He had offered hundreds of burnt offerings there in the past. That night the Lord appeared to him in a dream and asked him, "What would you like me to give you?" (1 Kings 3:3-5 GNB)

He became so wealthy by the empowerment of God's love.

You are the next in line for His profuse abundance.

"That night God appeared to Solomon and asked, "What would you like me to give you?" Solomon answered, "You always showed great love for my father David, and now you have let me succeed him as king. O Lord God, fulfil the promise you made to my father. You have made me king over a people who are so many that they cannot be counted, so give me the wisdom and knowledge I need to rule over them. Otherwise, how would I ever be able to rule this great people of yours?" God replied to Solomon, "You have made the right choice. Instead of asking for wealth or treasure or fame or the death of your enemies or even for long life for yourself, you have asked for wisdom and knowledge so that you can rule my people, over whom I have made you king. I will give you wisdom and knowledge. And in addition, I will give you more wealth, treasure, and fame than any king has ever had before or will ever have again." (2 Chronicles 1:7-12 GNB)

* Now, let us take a look at what Solomon did:
* He loved the Lord.
* He sacrificed; he gave beyond his best.
* He gave beyond his capability.
* He gave beyond his commitment.
* He gave beyond his dedication.

Nevertheless, if you are willing and obedient, God is able to do more than this for you.

He is raising in this end time, multi billionaires for His kingdom.

No matter what you have sacrificially given to His Kingdom, to His servant, to the needy and to the poor, God is able to multiply your seed a hundred fold.

"And Amaziah said to the man of God, But what shall we do for the hundred talents which I have given to the army of Israel? And the man of God answered, The Lord is able to give thee much more than this." (2 Chronicles 25:9 KJV

6. SET THE OPPRESSED AT LIBERTY

He has come to set free all those who are oppressed.

The seasons and the years the cankerworm, Palmer worm and caterpillar have stolen shall be restored and you shall be satisfied in the name of Jesus.

You will get back your liberty.

In greatness you will encounter greatness. He will comfort, ease and favour you without stress in the name of Jesus.

You shall no more be ashamed in Jesus name.

Look at what He says in *Matthew 8:17:*
"that it might be fulfilled which was spoken by Isaiah the prophet, saying: "He Himself took our infirmities And bore our sicknesses." (Matthew 8:17 NKJV)

No more diseases in the name of Jesus.

1 Peter 2:24:
"who Himself bore our sins in His own body on the tree, that

we, having died to sins, might live for righteousness by whose stripes you were healed." NKJV

"But the path of the just is like the shining sun, That shines ever brighter unto the perfect day." (Proverbs 4:18 NKJV)

Your path, destiny, glory, life, family, business etc shall shine brighter and brighter in the name of Jesus. You will go from story to glory, from lack to divine providence.

You will see Jesus in all that you do.

You will overcome your adversaries.

You will reign with Christ in this earth to the end. You were created to reign and to rule, you will take your rightful position in Jesus name. Is it not said concerning you in *Revelation 5:10:*
"And have made us kings and priests to our God; And we shall reign on the earth";

and in *Revelation 12:11:*
"And they overcame him by the blood of the Lamb and by the word of their testimony, and they did not love their lives to the death." (Revelation 12:11 NKJV)

You will overcome in the name of Jesus.

You will testify of the word of His grace.

You will triumph victoriously in the name of Jesus.

Your life will never be the same anymore; you will be better off in the name of Jesus.

You will manifest the fullness of your long awaited divine change as an individual, as a family, as a church, as a people, as a nation in Jesus mighty name.

Chapter Two

HOW TO ENHANCE AND MAXIMIZE THE BENEFITS OF THE DIVINE SETTLER

1. BE A MAN OF PEACE

The Divine Settler Himself is the Prince of peace, he tells us to: *"Follow peace with all men and holiness." Hebrews 12:14.*

Our God is the God of peace. His peace will keep you standing when others fall.

It is His peace that will keep your priorities in place, as you move towards your God-given goals.

Learn to place every situation into God's hands, and leave it there.

Isaiah 55:12 says; *"For ye shall go out with joy, and be led forth with peace: the mountains and the hills shall break forth before you into singing, and all the trees of the field shall clap their hands."*

God's peace is your compass. When the enemy tries to mislead you, the peace of God will guide you and keep you on the right path as long as you allow the peace of God to rule in your heart according to *Colossians 3:15 "Let the peace of God rule in your hearts..."*

Be careful not to entangle yourself in issues that are devoid of peace or not in line with the will of God.

Do not get into situations where God is not honored.

Do only what is pleasing to God, go only where He is glorified, and stay only where your heart is at peace.

The peace of God will abide with you and your household in Jesus name.

Trouble will be far from you.

Calamity will not come near your dwelling place.

The set time to celebrate your freedom from trouble has come.

The Settler Himself shall avenge your cause.

God will fight for you.

You will hold your peace.

The time to exhibit the unlimited possibilities of God's favour for you has come.

You will shine.

You will celebrate.

Your joy shall be full.

Concerning you and your family, there shall be no more mess.

No more marah (bitterness), hurt, malice, frustration, depression and resentment in Jesus name.

I command evil machinations to disappear from your life in the name of Jesus.

No more death.

No more struggles in the name of Jesus.

Phillipians. 2:9 says;
"Therefore God also has highly exalted Him and given Him the name which is above every name"

"Most assuredly, I say to you, he who believes in Me, the works that I do he will do also; and greater works than these he will do, because I go to My Father. And whatever you ask in My name, that I will do, that the Father may be glorified in the Son. If you ask anything in My name, I will do it." (John 14:12-14 NKJV)

You will encounter the strength of the Lord's salvation.

No more mourning but you will enjoy increase of comfort on all sides in Jesus name.

Receive Beauty for ashes.

Receive Oil of Joy for mourning.

Receive praise, blessing, power, riches, wisdom, strength, honour, glory in place of those heaviness in the name of Jesus.

Truly you will be a classified carrier of God's eternal glory. The Lord will be glorified in you, and in yours in the name of Jesus.

You will reign with Christ here on earth. It is said concerning you in *Revelation 5:10;*
"Nations shall call you blessed".

Families, neighbors, nations shall see the great mercy of The divine Settler in your life in the name of Jesus.

You will demonstrate in totality the reality of God's own tree of righteousness like never before in the name of Jesus.

You will be peculiar in power, in riches, in wisdom, in strength, in honour, in glory and in the blessings of God in the name of Jesus.

2. FORGIVE YOURSELF

Forgive yourself, forgive your past, and forgive those who did you wrong.

Ephesians 4:26 admonishes us not to allow the sun to go down on our wrath.

Never underestimate the power of forgiveness.

Holding bitterness and offenses only allows the devil to have a hold on you. You can't get forgiveness from God if you don't forgive others.

"For if ye forgive men their trespasses, your heavenly Father will also forgive you: But if ye forgive not men their trespasses, neither will your Father forgive your trespasses." (Matthew 6:14-15 KJV)

3. HAVE FAITH IN GOD

a. Trust in Him.
b. Have confidence in Him and His word.
c. Be courageous in acting as God's word is true.
d. Have the assurance that He cannot lie.
e. Act on His word without wavering.

Ephesians 6:16 says:
"Above all, taking the shield of faith, wherewith ye shall be able to quench all the fiery darts of the wicked".

Your faith in the ability of the living God will deliver results into your hands.

Jesus is the Door to our settlement. He says in *Matthew 16:18:*
" I will give unto thee the keys of the kingdom of heaven: and whatsoever thou shalt bind on earth shall be bound in heaven: and whatsoever thou shalt loose on earth shall be loosed in heaven ".

He can command all other doors to open.

He also said in *Matthew 17:20* that one of the keys to open doors on earth is the key of faith. The key of faith will either open doors for you manually or remotely.

Faith is the master key to settlement.

As you begin to apply the key of faith, the door of fruitfulness will open unto you.

The door of healing will open unto you.

The door of breakthrough, success, favour and unprecedented positive occurrences will open permanently unto you.

Apply the key of faith today and you will see great doors open!

4. BELIEVE GOD AND HIS WORD MORE THAN YOUR PROBLEMS.

Demonstrate it with your commitment, giving, utterance, obedience and service unto God and humanity. Serve Him without fear but in righteousness and holiness all the days of your life.

Study the word of God as you have never done because it will build in you more faith to access your miracles. The word of God is yea and amen. It has never failed and it will never fail.

Give more attention to God's word.

The God of settlement will visit you!

5. CAST ALL YOUR CARES UPON HIM AND BE ANXIOUS FOR NOTHING.

1 Peter 5:5-11:

"Likewise you younger people, submit yourselves to your elders. Yes, all of you be submissive to one another, and be clothed with humility, for "God resists the proud, But gives grace to the humble." Therefore humble yourselves under the Mighty hand of God, that He may exalt you in due time, casting all your care upon Him, for He cares for you. Be sober, be vigilant; because your adversary the devil walks about like a roaring lion, seeking whom he may devour. Resist him, steadfast in the faith, knowing that the same sufferings are experienced by your brotherhood in the world".

6. PRAY WITHOUT CEASING, FAST, DEVELOP AND EXERCISE FAITH.

Luke 11:1-13; Matthew 17:20-21; Hebrews 11:6.

"But may the God of all grace, who called us to His eternal glory by Christ Jesus, after you have suffered a while, perfect, establish, strengthen, and settle you. To Him be the glory and the dominion forever and ever."Amen. (I Peter 5:5-11 NKJV)

Chapter Three

HOW TO ACTIVATE
UNLIMITED SETTLEMENTS

"But may the God of all grace, who called us to His eternal glory by Christ Jesus, after you have suffered a while, perfect, establish, strengthen, and settle you."(I Peter 5:10 NKJV)

WHAT IS UNLIMITED SETTLEMENT?

Unlimited settlement can be defined as an extra ordinary event or development that is inexplicable by natural or scientific laws and is attributed to divine agency that brings about phenomenal divine occurrences.

HOW DO I ACTIVATE UNLIMITED SETTLEMENTS?

1. Know how to move God by praying fervently.

If you sincerely want to enjoy unlimited settlement, engage in: Fervent consistent prayers which includes praise and worship.

"Confess your faults one to another, and pray one for another, that ye may be healed. The effectual fervent prayer of a righteous man availeth much. Elias was a man subject to like passions as we are, and he prayed earnestly that it might not rain: and it rained not on the earth by the space of three years and six months." (James 5:16-17 KJV)

2. Fast consistently.

"And Jesus said unto them, Because of your unbelief: for verily I say unto you, If ye have faith as a grain of mustard seed, ye shall say unto this mountain, Remove hence to yonder place; and it shall remove; and nothing shall be impossible unto you. Howbeit this kind goeth not out but by prayer and fasting." *(Matthew 17:20-21 KJV)*

3. Hear and obey Godly instructions.

"I can of mine own self do nothing: as I hear, I judge: and my judgment is just; because I seek not mine own will, but the will of the Father which hath sent me." (John 5:30 KJV)

"And he that sent me is with me: the Father hath not left me alone; for I do always those things that please him." (John 8:29 KJV

4. Believe with unshakeable confidence and trust in God.

"And such as do wickedly against the covenant shall he corrupt by flatteries: but the people that do know their God shall be strong, and do exploits." Daniel 11:32 KJV

5. Develop a strong word base by studying, meditating and confessing the scriptures consistently.

"All scripture is given by inspiration of God, and is profitable for doctrine, for reproof, for correction, for instruction in righteousness". 2 Timothy 3:16 KJV

6. Get close to God as a sanctified believer.

Fellowship with the Holy Spirit consistently and passionately. A closer walk with God will make you know Him better.

"That I may know him, and the power of his resurrection, and the fellowship of his sufferings, being made conformable unto his death". (Philippians 3:10 KJV)

"To whom also he showed himself alive after his passion by many infallible proofs, being seen of them forty days, and speaking of the things pertaining to the kingdom of God" (Acts 1:3 KJV

You need to thirst more for God.

7. Show good hospitality to visitors.

Father Abraham enjoyed extraordinary settlement from God. He was sensitive to connect to collect.

"And the Lord appeared unto him in the plains of Mamre: and he sat in the tent door in the heat of the day; And he lift up his eyes and looked, and, lo, three men stood by him: and when he saw them, he ran to meet them from the tent door, and bowed himself toward the ground, And said, My Lord, if now I have found favour in thy sight, pass not away, I pray thee, from thy servant: Let a little water, I pray you, be fetched, and wash your feet, and rest yourselves under the tree: And I will fetch a morsel of bread, and comfort ye your hearts; after that ye shall pass on: for therefore are ye come to your servant. And they said, So do, as thou hast said." (Genesis 18:1-5 KJV)

Abraham had a visitation that brought a divine encounter.

You will not miss your visitation in Jesus name.

The helpers of your destiny will locate you for blessings.

When they come, you will not miss them in Jesus name.

8. Serve The Lord with your whole heart.

Give Him quality service. Serving God is the most rewarding venture one can engage in. God will adequately reward you for every quality service you render unto Him.

Give Jesus adequate honour and reverence. *(Malachi 1:6)*.

The Lord will reward your labour of love with heavenly blessings that cannot be compared to anything.

9. Be generous to God and mankind.

Another way to draw the attention of the Settler to yourself is through your generosity. Give good offerings to help the work of God. Remember that God loves a cheerful giver.

2 Corinthians 9:7 says; *"Every man according as he purposeth in his heart, so let him give; not grudgingly, or of necessity: for God loveth a cheerful giver. "*

You can also touch the heart of God through tithes, vows, covenant seeds and special offerings; through helping the poor and the needy.

The Lord will turn you around from struggling financially to stupendous financial abundance.

* Are you a consistent tither?
* Do you have challenges?
* Are you believing God for a child of your own?
* Perhaps you are seeking for a job.
* Is your problem that of a place to lay your head?
* Are you seeking and trusting God for healing?
* Or do you desire to get married?

Whatever your challenge is, God will visit you. He will

approve of you and visit you with miracles, signs and wonders.

If you are yet to give your life to Him, please do not hesitate or delay. Tomorrow might too late.

Every pending promise will be fulfilled in Jesus name.

"Through mighty signs and wonders, by the power of the Spirit of God; so that from Jerusalem, and round about unto Illyricum, I have fully preached the gospel of Christ." (Rom 15:19 KJV)

"And he said, If now I have found grace in thy sight, O Lord, my Lord, I pray thee, go among us; for it is a stiff necked people; and pardon our iniquity and our sin, and take us for thine inheritance. And he said, Behold, I make a covenant: before all thy people I will do marvels, such as have not been done in all the earth, nor in any nation: and all the people among which thou art shall see the work of the Lord: for it is a terrible thing that I will do with thee." (Exodus 34:9-10 KJV)

PRAY THESE PRAYER POINTS

1. Father, let me receive an uncommon settlement from you that will turn my life around.
2. Father, in my life, family, workplace, and ministry make me a recipient of your divine settlement.

WHY DO I NEED SETTLEMENT?

1. God settles So that people will believe in Him. *John 4:48*
2. He settles out of love and compassion for human suffering. *Luke 7:11-15*
3. To authenticate His "sent one" as a true servant of God. *Acts 2:22*
4. For us to develop strong faith in God. *Mark 11:23-24*
5. To turn hopelessness and desperate situations aright. *Ezekiel 37:1-14*

Why not give God a good reason to settle your case.

Be born again to win more of the compassion of God.

Be in total obedience to the word of God and have a strong faith in the name of Jesus.

Be a witness for Jesus (telling every one of His love, goodness and mercy).

God will notice your efforts, accept your person, open a book of remembrance on your case and give you a creative settlement in Jesus name.

Everyone faces problems in life but never allow them to separate you from God's divine destiny for your life.

1 Thessalonians 5:18 says *"in all things give thanks, this is the will of God for us all"*.

Romans 8:28 says *"All things work together for good for those who love God and are called according to His purpose"*.

Grace elected you, grace will see you through.

No matter what, keep praising, dancing, rejoicing, holding on to God and His promises irrespective of the problem you are going through; be it spiritual, marital or, financial, material, ministerial or academical.

You might be having challenges health wise, It could be rejection, depression, mental or psychological problems. Whatever it is, keep on believing, trusting and loving God extravagantly.

Jesus is Emmanuel: God with us; Grace with us.

Grace changes, restores, recovers all things but faith delivers what grace has paid for.

Without faith, it is impossible to please God.

It requires FAITH to recover all that grace paid for.

But faith can not be effective without developing the required working knowledge of His word.

So for faith to be effective, we need to get rid of our spiritual blindness.

God says, He will restore, He will overturn, He will revive. You will recover all and be satisfied.

I decree that your lost oil will be restored in the name of Jesus.

Your cutting edge will be restored.

Your lost axe head will be restored.

Your treasures, visions, dreams, destiny, purposes, goals, and aspirations will be restored.

Good people sometimes experience terrible problems.

Whatever problem you are encountering, The Settler will see you through in Jesus name.

In the Bible there are 3000 exceeding great and precious promises, custom designed in heaven to help us journey through the problems of life, and receive the supernatural provision available for each problem we encounter.

The challenge here is not the problem we are facing. How we conduct ourselves in the problem determines how long we will stay in it.

In *Genesis 45:4-5,7-8* Joseph was betrayed and sold into slavery by his blood brothers.

"And Joseph said unto his brethren, come near to me, I pray you. And they came near. And he said, I am Joseph your brother, whom ye sold into Egypt. Now therefore be not grieved, nor angry with yourselves, that ye sold me hither: for God did send me before you to preserve life".

In Genesis 50:20, he told his brothers ....
"But as for you, ye thought evil against me; but God meant it unto good, to bring to pass, as it is this day, to save much people alive." (Genesis 50:20 KJV)

Nevertheless, Joseph was faithful while going through the problems.

1. He maintained his character and integrity while enduring the problem. Maintain your Christian character and integrity even in your adversity.

2. He was patient throughout the duration of the problem. It is a matter of time, weeping may endure in the night, joy comes in the morning. Be Patient, your morning hour will soon be birthed. You will recover all in Jesus name.

3. He did not complain while facing ridicule, rejection, envy, dejection and jealousy. Be focused, stop moaning, complaining and murmuring because of what you are going through. You are just a step closer to your total recovery. You will recover all in Jesus name.

4. He held to his dream in the midst of lies and false accusations while in prison. Don't be embittered, malicious, disgruntled because of what you are going through. Hold on to your God given dreams and visions, it shall come to pass. Through it all, God showed favour to Joseph until the provision came. You will recover all, in Jesus name.

5. Joseph had the vision to see the reason why he had to go through his problem. So learn to see the purpose of your problem and declare the end from the beginning.

6. Even though Joseph spent years in the problem , he never stopped listening to the voice of God. Keep hearing God without ceasing. Don't forsake your fellowship with God and with brethren. Be committed like never before.

7. Joseph remained faithful to God and God remained faithful to him, leading him to the divine purpose for which he was created.

You will recover all!

The beggar at the gate of the temple walked, leaped for joy and kept giving praise to God.

Your situations, circumstances, needs, wants, etc will leap for joy in Jesus name.

Your vat will bring forth wine in abundance.

Increase of oil, hidden treasures, wealth transfer will be yours.

You will get back seven times everything the palmer worm, cankerworm, and caterpillar might have stolen from you.

You will yet win again and again.

You will laugh a better laughter. You will surprise those who thought your joy will be short lived.

For you, it is going to be a better beginning, a new life, the dawning of a new season.

Welcome into your year of Extravagant Grace!

You will divinely recover all, in Jesus mighty name.

Chapter Five

PRAYER POINTS TO DIVINELY SETTLE THE ISSUES OF LIFE

DIVINE RECOVERY

1. Wind of God, drive away every power of the ungodly rising against my destiny, in the name of Jesus.
2. In this season of divine restoration, O God, be the glory and the lifter of my head, in the name of Jesus.
3. Oh gates blocking my blessings, be lifted up in Jesus name.
4. Any organ of my body that has lost its function, resume your functions now, in the name of Jesus.
5. My benefits of Grace manifest now, in the name of Jesus.
6. Ask the God of all possibilities to settle you. Say the following boldly:

with :
* Settle me with Your Spirit.
* Settle me with Your glory.
* Settle me with Your presence.
* Settle me with Your blessings.
* Settle me with Your favour.
* Settle me with Your power.
* Settle me with Your miracles, signs, wonders and strange acts.

* Settle me with Your ways.
* Settle me with Your wisdom, understanding and revelation knowledge.
* Settle me with the total package of Your divine settlements, in the name of Jesus.

7. O Lord glorify Your name in my life, family, business, ministry, city, state and nation in the name of Jesus.

DIVINE HELP

"Lord, heal me and I will be completely well; rescue me and I will be perfectly safe. You are the one I praise! The people say to me, "Where are those threats the Lord made against us? Let him carry them out now!" But, Lord, I never urged you to bring disaster on them; I did not wish a time of trouble for them. Lord, you know this; you know what I have said. Do not be a terror to me; you are my place of safety when trouble comes. Bring disgrace on those who persecute me, but spare me, Lord. Fill them with terror, but do not terrify me. Bring disaster on them and break them to pieces" (Jeremiah 17:14-18 GNB)

1. O Lord, heal me, my family, my business, my finances, my ministry etc in the name of Jesus.
2. O Lord keep us perfectly safe in the name of Jesus.
3. O Lord do not be a terror to me for You are my place of safety, in the name of Jesus.
4. O Lord bring disgrace on those who persecute me but spare me, in Jesus name.
5. O Lord avenge my cause but spare me and all my interests, in the name of Jesus
6. Sovereign Lord, in Your mercy, send me help round about and fulfill Your goodness in my life, family, business, career and ministry in the name of Jesus.

7. Sovereign Lord, according to Your majestic power, might, wonders and deeds, restore my inheritance fully and lift me higher in the name of Jesus.

"Listen, Jeremiah! Everyone in this land; the kings of Judah, the officials, the priests, and the people will be against you. But today I am giving you the strength to resist them; you will be like a fortified city, an iron pillar, and a bronze wall. They will not defeat you, for I will be with you to protect you. I, the Lord, have spoken." (Jeremiah 1:18-19 GNB)

8. O Lord, grant me the grace to resist those who stand against me and Your purpose for my destiny in the name of Jesus.
9. O Lord, arise, stand, protect and preserve me with all my interests in Jesus name.
10. Sovereign Lord, take not Your help away from me, in the name of Jesus.

"I myself will teach your people, and give them prosperity and peace. Justice and right will make you strong. You will be safe from oppression and terror. Whoever attacks you does it without my consent; whoever fights against you will fall. "I create the blacksmith, who builds a fire and forges weapons. I also create the soldier, who uses the weapons to kill. But no weapon will be able to hurt you; you will have an answer for all who accuse you. I will defend my servants and give them victory." The Lord has spoken. (Isaiah 54:13-17 GNB)

11. O Lord, teach me to abide in Your peace and prosperity in the name of Jesus.
12. O Lord, deliver me and my interests from oppression and terror in the name of Jesus.
13. Sovereign Lord, ensure that whoever fights me and my

interests fall woefully in the name of Jesus.

14. O Lord, let no weapon be able to hurt me and all my interests in the name of Jesus.

15. O Lord, grant me answers and victory concerning all who accuse me, in the name of Jesus.

"I look to the mountains; where will my help come from? My help will come from the Lord, who made heaven and earth. He will not let you fall; your protector is always awake. The protector of Israel never dozes or sleeps. The Lord will guard you; he is by your side to protect you. The sun will not hurt you during the day, nor the moon during the night. The Lord will protect you from all danger; he will keep you safe. He will protect you as you come and go now and for ever". (Psalm 121:1-8 GNB)

16. O Lord, help me not to fall! Send me help speedily from above in the name of Jesus.

17. O Lord, protect from me all danger; keep me safe for ever in the name of Jesus.

18. O Lord, let no sun or moon smite me and all my interests in the name of Jesus.

19. O Lord, in my going out and my coming in; be my guide and shield, all the days of my life in the name of Jesus.

20. O Lord, I place a demand for Your everlasting help in life, ministry and destiny in the name of Jesus.

"When Jesus entered Capernaum, a Roman officer met him and begged for help: "Sir, my servant is sick in bed at home, unable to move and suffering terribly." "I will go and make him well," Jesus said. "Oh no, sir," answered the officer. "I do not deserve to have you come into my house. Just give the order, and

my servant will get well. I, too, am a man under the authority of superior officers, and I have soldiers under me. I order this one, 'Go!' and he goes; and I order that one, 'Come!' and he comes; and I order my slave, 'Do this!' and he does it." When Jesus heard this, he was surprised and said to the people following him, "I tell you, I have never found anyone in Israel with faith like this. I assure you that many will come from the east and the west and sit down with Abraham, Isaac, and Jacob at the feast in the Kingdom of heaven. But those who should be in the Kingdom will be thrown out into the darkness, where they will cry and grind their teeth." Then Jesus said to the officer, "Go home, and what you believe will be done for you." And the officer's servant was healed that very moment." (Matthew 8:5-13 GNB)

21. O Lord, just give the order and all that concerns me and my interests shall be totally settled in the name of Jesus.
22. Father, help me and all my interests to be partaker of the feast in the kingdom of Heaven in the name of Jesus.

CHANGE OF STORY TO GLORY.

"There was a man named Jabez, who was the most respected member of his family. His mother had given him the name Jabez, because his birth had been very painful. But Jabez prayed to the God of Israel, "Bless me, God, and give me much land. Be with me and keep me from anything evil that might cause me pain." And God gave him what he prayed for. (1 Chronicles 4:9-10 GNB)

1. Thank You Father for changing our story to glory in the name of Jesus. *(2 Corinthians 3:18)*

2. Father, bless me, my spouse, my children and my family beyond what human beings can comprehend in the name of Jesus. *(1 Corinthians 2:9)*

3. Father, give unto me much land, wealth and riches in the name of Jesus. *(Psalm 24:1; Deuteronomy 8:18; Ephesians 1:3)*

4. Father, be with me and keep me from anything evil that might pain me in the name of Jesus. *(Isaiah 57:21)*

5. Father, You granted Jabez all what he asked for, O Lord do exceeding abundantly above all I have asked of You in the name of Jesus. *(Ephesians 3:20)*

6. Father, exercise Your supernatural wisdom for great riches, wealth, greatness and comfort in all my endeavors in the name of Jesus.

"Before long I will shake heaven and earth, land and sea. I will overthrow all the nations, and their treasures will be brought here, and the Temple will be filled with wealth. All the silver and gold of the world is mine. The new Temple will be more splendid than the old one, and there I will give my people prosperity and peace." The Lord Almighty has spoken. (Haggai 2:6-9 GNB)

The Lord says, "Can't you see what has happened to you? Before you started to rebuild the Temple, you would go to a heap of corn expecting to find 200 kilogrammes, but there would be only a hundred. You would go to draw a hundred litres of wine from a vat, but find only forty. I sent scorching winds and hail to ruin everything you tried to grow, but still you did not repent. Today is the 24th day of the ninth month, the day that the foundation of the Temple has been completed. See what is going to happen from now on. Although there is no corn left, and the grapevines, fig trees, pomegranates, and olive trees

have not yet produced, yet from now on I will bless you."
(Haggai 2:15-19 GNB)

7. Father, as You shake the heaven, earth, land, sea and overthrow the nations, fill my life, my family, my ministry, and the church with abundance of treasures, wealth and riches in the name of Jesus.

8. Father, give unto us abundance of prosperity, blessings, joy and peace as an individual, a family, church, ministry and nation by Your divine shift in the name of Jesus. *(Numbers 11:31)*

9. Father, from henceforth bless my seed sown and labour of love exceeding mightily in the name of Jesus. *(2 Corinthians 8:9; 9:8)*

10. Father, advertise Your blessedness and greatness in our life, family, destiny and assignments exceeding greatly in the name of Jesus. *(Psalms 71:21;1:3)*

11. Father, wherever I have erred as an individual, family, church, people or nation remember the blood of Jesus and the price paid at calvary; forgive and restore greater glory and prosperity than ever before now in the name of Jesus *(Amos 4:4-13;1 John1:9; Romans 5:17)*

12. Father, remember that mercy surpasses judgement; let Your sovereign love prevail in my situation, family, congregation, assignments and nation in the name of Jesus. *(James 2:13)*

13. Father, do great and mighty wonders in my life, family and works to reflect Your mercy and divine shift for good in the name of Jesus. *(Acts 2:22)*

14. Father, You are the Almighty, do mighty glory, - blessings, victories, prosperity in my life, family, assignments and nation in the name of Jesus.

15. Father, let there be remarkable positive Divine Shift in

my story to glory honorably in the name of Jesus. *(Isaiah 61:6-7)*

16. Father, grant me provisions, treasures and proofs that are inexplicable naturally to establish Your presence in my life, family, ministry etc in the name of Jesus. *(Psalms 16 :11; 23:1; Philippians 4:19)*

17. Father, change my "divine signet" to that which cannot be contested, insulted, resisted or confronted by any power or spirit in the name of Jesus. *(Matthew 16:19; 8:8-9).*

18. Father, as I call on You, fill my desires with Your passion, dreams, visions, proofs, benefits etc so that I will lack nothing in the name of Jesus. *(Psalm 23:1)*

"I saw someone riding a red horse. He had stopped among some myrtle trees in a valley, and behind him were other horses red, dappled, and white. I asked him, "Sir, what do these horses mean?" He answered, "I will show you what they mean. The Lord sent them to go and inspect the earth." They reported to the angel: "We have been all over the world and have found that the whole world lies helpless and subdued." Then the angel said, "Almighty Lord, you have been angry with Jerusalem and the cities of Judah for seventy years now. How much longer will it for Jerusalem, my holy city, and I am very. (Zechariah 1:18-21).

19. Father, as You inspect the earth, remember us and save us in Your mercy and goodness in the name of Jesus.

20. Father, in Your mercy, send forth Your comforting Angel to vindicate and bring forth our prosperity as individuals, family, people, nation, church that are called by Your name in the name of Jesus.

21. Father, visit us and deliver us from nations and leaders

that have scattered us; economically, financially, materially, etc in the name of Jesus.

22. Father, we receive new wine in all our endeavors in the name of Jesus.

23. Father, open unto me windows and doors of Joy in the name of Jesus.

24. According to Your word in Deuteronomy 1:11, Father, make me a thousand times more; spiritually, financially, economically, materially, physically, ministerially, maritally, academically, biologically, monetarily, project wise, in the name of Jesus.

YOU WILL NOT DIE!

Make the following declarations boldly and loudly by faith:
"I shall not die, but live, and declare the works of the Lord."
(Psalm 118:17 KJV)

"He that dwelleth in the secret place of the most High shall abide under the shadow of the Almighty. I will say of the Lord, He is my refuge and my fortress: my God; in him will I trust. Surely he shall deliver thee from the snare of the fowler, and from the noisome pestilence. He shall cover thee with his feathers, and under his wings shalt thou trust: his truth shall be thy shield and buckler. Thou shalt not be afraid for the terror by night; nor for the arrow that flieth by day; Nor for the pestilence that walketh in darkness; nor for the destruction that wasteth at noonday. A thousand shall fall at thy side, and ten thousand at thy right hand; but it shall not come nigh thee. Only with thine eyes shalt thou behold and see the reward of the wicked. Because thou hast made the Lord, which is my refuge, even the most High, thy habitation; There shall no evil befall thee, neither shall any plague come nigh thy dwelling. For he shall

give his angels charge over thee, to keep thee in all thy ways. They shall bear thee up in their hands, lest thou dash thy foot against a stone. Thou shalt tread upon the lion and adder: the young lion and the dragon shalt thou trample under feet. Because he hath set his love upon me, therefore will I deliver him: I will set him on high, because he hath known my name. He shall call upon me, and I will answer him: I will be with him in trouble; I will deliver him, and honour him. With long life will I satisfy him, and shew him my salvation." (Psalm 91:1-16 KJV)

I decree and declare that the remaining days of this year, I shall not bury anyone before his/her time and I shall not be buried in Jesus name.

Psalm 118 :17 assures me and my family that we will not die but live to declare the works of the Lord in Jesus name.

No accident shall befall us in Jesus name.

Arrows of sudden death fashioned against me and my family, gather hundred fold STRENGTH, go back and prosper in the lives of your senders in Jesus name, because *Isaiah 54:17* says, *"no weapon fashioned against me shall prosper and every tongue that rises against me in judgement I shall condemn".*

The Lord will cover our heads in the days of battle throughout, in the mighty name of Jesus.

As The Lord lives, I shall live with my family to fulfill destiny in Jesus name.

No pestilence nor plague shall come near our dwelling places, in the Name of Jesus.

NOW PRAY THE FOLLOWING PRAYER POINTS AGGRESSIVELY:

1. Thank God for the power over death through our Lord Jesus Christ. *Romans 5:10 "For if, when we were enemies, we were reconciled to God by the death of his Son, much more, being reconciled, we shall be saved by his life."*

"I am crucified with Christ: nevertheless I live; yet not I, but Christ liveth in me: and the life which I now live in the flesh I live by the faith of the Son of God, who loved me, and gave himself for me." (Galatians 2:20KJV)

2. I release my destiny and that of my household from the hold of sudden death in Jesus name.

"Verily I say unto you, Whatsoever ye shall bind on earth shall be bound in heaven: and whatsoever ye shall loose on earth shall be loosed in heaven"(Matthew 18:18 KJV)

"Thou shalt also decree a thing, and it shall be established unto thee: and the light shall shine upon thy ways." (Job 22:28 KJV)

3. All attempts of plagues, sicknesses, diseases made against me and my family be aborted in Jesus name.

"Surely he hath borne our griefs, and carried our sorrows: yet we did esteem him stricken, smitten of God, and afflicted. But he was wounded for our transgressions, he was bruised for our iniquities: the chastisement of our peace was upon him; and with his stripes we are healed." (Isaiah 53:4-5 KJV)

"That it might be fulfilled which was spoken by Esaias the

prophet, saying, Himself took our infirmities, and bare our sicknesses." (Matthew 8:17 KJV)

4. I withdraw my name and that of my family members from the register of untimely death in Jesus name.
5. Satanic grave dug for me and my family, swallow your diggers in Jesus name.

"Thou shalt come to thy grave in a full age, like as a shock of corn cometh in his season. "(Job 5:26 KJV)

6. Every wicked personality preparing coffins for me , be it in the past, present times, and in the future, enter into your coffins in Jesus name.
7. My life and that of my loved ones will not be aborted before my God ordained time in Jesus name.
8. Every satanic extinguishers of destiny fashioned against me and my family, I dismantle you, in Jesus name.
9. My star and that of my family will not be cut short in the name of Jesus.

"Saying, Arise, and take the young child and his mother, and go into the land of Israel: for they are dead which sought the young child's life." (Matthew 2:20 KJV)

"Saying, Where is he that is born King of the Jews? for we have seen his star in the east, and are come to worship him. Saying, Arise, and take the young child and his mother, and go into the land of Israel: for they are dead which sought the young child's life." (Matthew 2:2,20 KJV)

10. Every door of untimely death opened to satan by me or any of my family members, or my ancestors, I close it by the blood of Jesus.

11. Every evil consultation going on anywhere to cut my life short or that of any of my family members, be abolished by the blood of Jesus.

12. O Lord, release my life and that of my family from any negative prophecy and evil predictions of premature death in Jesus name.

13. I break and loose myself and my family from all hidden evil covenants and vows of premature death, in Jesus name.

14. Every evil thought and plans to harm or kill me or any of my family members, be aborted by the blood of Jesus, in Jesus name.

15. I declare that I will not die but live to declare the works of The Lord in the land of the living.

16. By the blood of Jesus and His mercy, I break every evil covenant linkage with plagues, sickness, diseases, death and hell in the name of Jesus.

"And they overcame him by the blood of the Lamb, and by the word of their testimony; and they loved not their lives unto death." (Revelation 12:11 KJV)

17. I release my length of days and that of my family from evil covenants in Jesus name

"There shall no evil befall thee, neither shall any plague come nigh thy dwelling" (Psalm91:10 KJV)

18. Every evil altar of death and hell erected against me and my family, be dismantled in Jesus name.

19. I declare my right to live according to *Romans 8:1-2:*

"There is therefore no condemnation to me who is in Christ Jesus, who walk not after the flesh, but after the Spirit. For the

law of the Spirit of life in Christ has made me free from the law of sin and death "

20. This year will not end at the expense of my blood in the name of Jesus.

"Thou crownest the year with thy goodness; and thy paths drop fatness." (Psalm 65:11 KJV)

21. Whatever is giving me comfort will not kill me in Jesus name. (Car, Airplane, Train, Ferry, Ship, Electricity, Water, Air, Foods, Drinks, Building, Jobs, Money, e.t.c)

22. By the blood of Jesus and His everlasting mercy, I renew my divine insurance against mysterious death, sicknesses, diseases, plagues, sorrow, tragedy, and spiritual attacks, in the name of Jesus.

23. Angels of life, maintain security around me and my family at all times in the name of Jesus .

24. O Lord, prevent me and my family from making any journey of no return in the name of Jesus.

25. I decree that the remaining days of this year for me and my family, there shall be no sorrow and tragedy in the name of Jesus.

26. I cover myself and my family with the blood of Jesus.

27. For the rest of the year, I will not weep In Jesus name.

28. For the rest of the year, i reject contrary winds, evil and mysterious winds in Jesus name.

29. I reject "had I known" in the remaining days of the year, in the name of Jesus.

30. For the rest of the year, I will not fail or flutter in the name of Jesus.

31. For the rest of the year, I will prosper and live in good health in Jesus name.

32. For the rest of the year, I will move forward in the name of Jesus.

33. For the rest of the year I become unstoppable to make a difference in the name of Jesus.

34. For the rest of the year, I reject every form of attack in the name of Jesus.

35. For the rest of the year, I reject accident, death, robbery attack, assassination, evil arrows, sicknesses, diseases, harassment, dream attacks and pollutions in the name of Jesus.

36. For the rest of the year, I shall not fade away in Jesus name.

37. For the rest of the year, my star shall not fade away, in Jesus name.

38. In the remaining days of the year, my sun will not set suddenly in Jesus name.

39. Throughout this year, my heaven will not close suddenly, in the name of Jesus.

40. Throughout this year, my moon will not go dark ,in the name of Jesus.

41. Throughout this year, my life will not turn upside down in the name of Jesus.

42. I shall not suffer any regrets in the name of Jesus.

43. I reject mistakes and errors in the name of Jesus.

44. I shall not be mistaken for evil in the name of Jesus.

45. Powers of darkness will not capture me and members of my family in Jesus name.

46. No strange sickness, disease, or plague will strike me and my family members in Jesus name.

47. I will not go blind in Jesus name.

48. I reject paralysis in Jesus name.

49. I reject the spirit of wheel chair in Jesus name.

50. I reject the spirit of mortuary in the name of Jesus.
51. I reject the spirit of prison in Jesus name.
52. I reject the spirit of burial ground in Jesus name
53. I reject the spirit of madness in the name of Jesus.
54. I reject the spirit of failure in the name of Jesus.
55. I reject the spirit of poverty in Jesus name.
56. I reject the spirit of delay in the name of Jesus.
57. I reject the spirit of downfall in Jesus name.
58. I reject the spirit of indebtedness in Jesus name.
59. I reject the spirit of remaining in the same old ways in Jesus name.
60. I reject the spirit of hardship in Jesus name.
61. I reject the spirit of embargo in Jesus name.
62. I reject the spirit of disaster in Jesus name.
63. I reject the Spirit of barrenness in Jesus name.
64. I reject the spirit of hatred without reasons in Jesus name.
65. I reject the spirit of disappointment in Jesus name.
66. I reject the spirit of nakedness in Jesus name.
67. I reject the spirit of labouring without results in Jesus name.
68. I reject the spirit of harvest failure in Jesus name.
69. I reject the spirit of progress abortion in the name of Jesus.
70. I reject the spirit of negative prophecies in Jesus name.
71. I reject the spirit of rejection in the name of Jesus.
72. I reject the spirit of misfortune in the name of Jesus.
73. I reject the spirit of depression in the name of Jesus.
74. I reject the spirit of suicide in Jesus name.
75. I will not wear rags, and sudden downfall will not be my portion in Jesus name.
76. I shall succeed in all areas in Jesus name.

77. My fortune shall rise up in Jesus name.
78. God will bless my coming in and my going out in Jesus name.
79. My position shall not be vacant in Jesus name.
80. Enemies of progress will not laugh at me in Jesus name.
81. My life shall attract miracles, goodness, progress and blessings in Jesus name.
82. I will not die in my sleep in Jesus name.
83. I will not bury anyone young and they will not bury me in Jesus name.
84. Doors of opportunity will open unto me in the name of Jesus.
85. I will arise and shine in Jesus name.
86. All my good dreams shall come to pass in Jesus name.
87. I will overcome all problems and trials in Jesus name.
88. I shall not be an object of ridicule or mockery in Jesus name.
89. My helpers will not die in Jesus name.
90. The Lord will remember me for good in Jesus name.
91. Whatever I lay my hands on shall prosper in Jesus name.
92. In the remaining days of the year, anointing for overflowing prosperity shall fall on me in Jesus name.
93. The Lord will renovate my life and works with blessings, favour and mercy in Jesus name.
94. All my divine helpers shall locate me and help me In Jesus name.
95. All the good things I see in my dreams shall come to pass in Jesus name.
96. O Lord, I reject negative answers from wherever I am expecting positive answers in Jesus name.

97. Father, deliver me from mistakes that can hinder my blessings in Jesus name.

98. In the remaining days of the year, O Lord, give me miracles that will generate argument among those who know me before now in Jesus name.

99. Father, hurry up to help me in Jesus name.

100. Father, do new things that are outstanding in my life and works in Jesus name.

101. Father, I give You thanks, praise, worship, glory for who You are, all You are doing and will still do in my life and works in Jesus name.

RICH HARVEST

"What a rich harvest your goodness provides! Wherever you go there is plenty." (Psalm 65:11 GNT)

"Lord, I look up to you, up to heaven, where you rule. As a servant depends on his master, as a maid depends on her mistress, so we will keep looking to you, O Lord our God, until you have mercy on us. Be merciful to us, Lord, be merciful; we have been treated with so much contempt. We have been mocked too long by the rich and scorned by proud oppressors." (Psalm 123:1-4 GNT)

1. O Lord, let all of creation be competing to favor me and my family members in the name of Jesus.

2. O Lord, let the rivers of multiple income and cash locate me, flow into me, my business and ministry in the name of Jesus.

3. O Lord, let people and resources assigned to move me forward appear and locate me now, in the name of Jesus.

4. O Lord, let the people and the resources assigned for

my breakthroughs manifest in my life now, in the name of Jesus.

5. Let all my resources and cash anywhere in creation come to me.

"Thus saith the Lord, the Holy One of Israel, and his Maker, Ask me of things to come concerning my sons, and concerning the work of my hands command ye me. "(Isaiah 45:11 KJV)

6. Every mysterious force hindering my breakthroughs, die in Jesus name.

7. O Lord, connect me to the network of the rich and the wealthy in Jesus name.

"You let people ride over our heads; we went through fire and water, but you brought us to a place of abundance." (Psalm 66:12 NIV)

8. O Lord, connect me to those that will transfer wealth to me in Jesus name.

9. O Lord, let the rich, wealthy, and the powerful be competing to favor me in Jesus name.

10. My financial star shall arise and shine in Jesus name.

"Arise, shine; for thy light is come, and the glory of the Lord is risen upon thee." (Isaiah 60:1 KJV)

11. Powers blocking my financial breakthroughs, be uprooted in Jesus name.

"For I will not see you now by the way; but I trust to tarry a while with you, if the Lord permit. But I will tarry at Ephesus until Pentecost. For a great door and effectual is opened unto me, and there are many adversaries." (1 Corinthians 16:7-9 KJV)

12. Wealth and riches of the wicked be transferred to me in Jesus name.

13. Wealth of the unrighteous, I transfer you into my hands by fire by power in the name of Jesus.

14. Barriers to my financial breakthrough, be consumed by fire and thunder in the name of Jesus.

15. Barriers to the wealth transfer of the wicked to me, be consumed by fire in Jesus name

16. I uproot forces of delay and hold up to my financial and material breakthroughs in the name of Jesus.

17. Satanic police arresting the transfer of finances to me, DIE in Jesus name.

18. Forces of delay working against the transfer of finances to me, DIE in Jesus name.

19. By the blood of Jesus, satanic orders against the transfer of finances to me be cancelled, in the name of Jesus.

20. Father, let every distance between me and my financial breakthroughs be removed, in the name of Jesus.

"And it came to pass in the mean while, that the heaven was black with clouds and wind, and there was a great rain. And Ahab rode, and went to Jezreel. And the hand of the Lord was on Elijah; and he girded up his loins, and ran before Ahab to the entrance of Jezreel. "(1 Kings 18:45-46KJV)

21. O Lord, let financial wealth and riches be transferred to me without ceasing in the name of Jesus.

22. O Lord, let the hand of the Lord come upon me for financial and material transfers speedily in Jesus name.

23. All my labors shall be rewarded in Jesus name.

24. My financial seeds shall bring forth exceeding great harvest in Jesus name.

25. I will not lack (spiritual, material, human and financial) resources in the name of Jesus.
26. I will be blessed with money and material blessings in abundance in Jesus name.
27. I prophecy by the decree of heaven that every day shall be heaven on earth for me and my family, in the name of Jesus.
28. The rich and wealthy will favour me with gifts in Jesus name.
29. I will be given unsolicited gifts and cash, in the name of Jesus.
30. I will be treated with dignity and accorded with honor everywhere that I go in Jesus name.
31. CASH will be transferred and deposited into my accounts mysteriously, in the name of Jesus.
32. The wicked will work very hard to make money to hand over to me, in the name of Jesus.
33. I will be blessed with real estates, houses, cars, assets, provisions and every good thing in life, in the name of Jesus.

"The Lord our God spake unto us in Horeb, saying, Ye have dwelt long enough in this mount: Turn you, and take your journey, and go to the mount of the Amorites, and unto all the places nigh there unto, in the plain, in the hills, and in the vale, and in the south, and by the sea side, to the land of the Canaanites, and unto Lebanon, unto the great river, the river Euphrates. Behold, I have set the land before you: go in and possess the land which the Lord sware unto your fathers, Abraham, Isaac, and Jacob, to give unto them and to their seed after them. And I spake unto you at that time, saying, I am not able to bear you myself alone: The Lord your God hath

multiplied you, and, behold, ye are this day as the stars of heaven for multitude. (The Lord God of your fathers make you a thousand times so many more as ye are, and bless you, as he hath promised you!) "(Deuteronomy 1:6-11 KJV)

34. My breakthrough shall be spectacular. It will affect my generation forever in Jesus name.

35. I will reap favourably where I have not labored, in the name of Jesus.

36. Heaven will arrange and coordinate breakthroughs for me.

37. It shall be sweeter than the honey comb for me and my family, in the name of Jesus.

38. My breakthrough will not be hindered in the name of Jesus.

39. The glory of my voice shall be heard globally, in the name of Jesus.

40. O Lord, enlarge my coast and bless me indeed in the name of Jesus.

"And Jabez was more honourable than his brethren: and his mother called his name Jabez, saying, Because I bare him with sorrow. And Jabez called on the God of Israel, saying, Oh that thou wouldest bless me indeed, and enlarge my coast, and that thine hand might be with me, and that thou wouldest keep me from evil, that it may not grieve me! And God granted him that which he requested". (1 Chronicles 4:9-10 KJV)

41. My ministry shall be in demand globally in the name of Jesus.

42. Heaven will create opportunities for me on earth in the name of Jesus.

"Moreover the profit of the earth is for all: the king himself is

served by the field. "(Ecclesiastes 5:9 KJV)

"I returned, and saw under the sun, that the race is not to the swift, nor the battle to the strong, neither yet bread to the wise, nor yet riches to men of understanding, nor yet favour to men of skill; but time and chance happeneth to them all." (Ecclesiastes 9:11 KJV)

43. Angels (celestial and human) of blessings locate me now, in the name of Jesus.
44. My messengers (celestial and human) of joy and prosperity seek me and find me always, in the name of Jesus.
45. Wise men and women bearing financial and material gifts shall locate me in the name of Jesus.

"Saying, Where is he that is born King of the Jews? for we have seen his star in the east, and are come to worship him."

"When they had heard the king, they departed; and, lo, the star, which they saw in the east, went before them, till it came and stood over where the young child was. When they saw the star, they rejoiced with exceeding great joy. And when they were come into the house, they saw the young child with Mary his mother, and fell down, and worshipped him: and when they had opened their treasures, they presented unto him gifts; gold, and frankincense, and myrrh. "(Matthew 2:2; 9-11 KJV)

46. People in high places will arise and help me in the name of Jesus.
47. My star will arise and shine brighter than ever before, in the name of Jesus Christ.

"But the path of the just is as the shining light, that shines more and more unto the perfect day." (Proverbs 4:18 KJV)

48. Satanic police arresting the transfer of good things and finances to me, die in Jesus name.

49. Forces delaying the transfer of finances to me, die in Jesus name.

"Then the angel I had seen standing on the sea and on the land raised his right hand to heaven. And he swore by him who lives for ever and ever, who created the heavens and all that is in them, the earth and all that is in it, and the sea and all that is in it, and said, "There will be no more delay!"(Revelation 10:5-6 NIV)

50. By the blood of Jesus, I cancel every satanic order against transfer of wealth to me. All the days of my life, the rich and wealthy will seek for me with their treasures

51. Let the Hand of the Lord upon my financial transactions come through speedily in the name of Jesus. My labors shall be rewarded.

* My financial seeds shall yield abundant financial harvests

* I will not lack materially and financially in the name of Jesus.

* I will be blessed with money and material blessings in abundance.

* I prophecy by the decree of heaven that the 365 days of the year shall be days of heaven on earth for me and my family, in the name of Jesus.

* Rich and wealthy men and women will entreat me with gifts.

* I will be given unsolicited gifts and cash exceeding abundantly, in the name of Jesus.

* I will be treated with dignity and accorded with honor everywhere that I go this year in Jesus name.
* CASH will be transferred and deposited into my accounts mysteriously.
* The wicked will work very hard to make money and hand them over to me.
* My breakthrough shall be spectacular. It will affect my generation forever in Jesus name.
* I will reap where I have not labored. Heaven will arrange and coordinate breakthroughs for me and my family.
* This year shall be sweeter than the honey comb for me and my family.

Thank You Lord because I know You have answered me. *1 John 5:14-15.*

RE-BRANDING FOR SUPERNATURAL IMPACT

1. O Lord , show me Your mercy.
2. Let every wicked horn be destroyed in Jesus name. *(Zechariah 1:17-19)*
3. O Lord have mercy on me not to abort Your purpose for my life and destiny in the name of Jesus.
4. O Lord, grant me the boldness and the passion to pursue Your kingdom agenda for my destiny without ceasing in the name of Jesus.
5. I come against every form of fear in the name of Jesus. *(2 Timothy 1:7)*
6. O Lord, send me helpers so as to fulfill destiny in the name of Jesus.
7. Father, grant unto me upward and forward movement (spiritually, financially, materially, ministerially,

mentally, numerically, internationally, etc) without delay in the name of Jesus. *(Exodus 14:10-15)*

8. My Lord and my God, turn things around in my favour, in the name of Jesus.

9. Father, finish every incomplete project in my life, family, ministry and destiny, gloriously in my favour in the name of Jesus.

10. O Lord, grant unto me divine answers and directions to every question in my heart as regards the affairs of my life, my ministry, family and destiny in the name of Jesus.

11. O Lord, re-brand me entirely in my spirit, soul and body in the name of Jesus.

12. O Lord, use me for the promotion and victory of all You bring across my path without delay, in the name of Jesus.

13. O Lord, uphold my hands perpetually with Your right hand of righteousness without ceasing in the name of Jesus: help me not to fail.

    *   I put my legs on Your legs...
    *   I put my head on Your head...
    *   Let me not fail because You never fail.
    *   Let me not fall for You never fall.

14. Holy Ghost fire fall on me, in the name of Jesus.

15. Holy Ghost fire, enter into me in the name of Jesus.

16. Holy Ghost fire, fill me with apostolic authority, divine utterances, signs, wonders, strange acts, blessings, deliverance, liftings, breakthroughs more than that of the early church in the name of Jesus.

17. O Lord, quench my thirst with Your power for signs, wonders, miracles, and blessings in the name of Jesus.

18. O Lord, send down fire that cannot be resisted or

insulted with divine proofs in the name of Jesus.

19. Father, give unto me new testimonies that are unprecedented, strange, new, mighty; that cannot be covered, or denied in the name of Jesus.

20. I and my children are for signs and wonders. O Lord, endorse it completely in our favour in the name of Jesus.

21. O Lord, release upon us unusual testimonies that cannot be shared alone in Jesus name.

22. O Lord, show Yourself strong and mighty in all my endeavors in the name of Jesus.

23. O Lord, take me to the core of the ocean of good success, greatness, wealth and blessings in the name of Jesus.

24. O Lord, build glorious mansion for me physically in the name of Jesus.

25. I decree I will no more struggle or suffer loss any more in Jesus name. I decree:
  * No more shame.
  * No more pains.
  * No more lack.
  * No more agony.
  * No more wastage.
  * No more stagnation.
  * No more defeat.
  * No more sickness.
  * No more disease in the name of Jesus.

26. O Lord, change my level of impact beyond human comprehension and limitations in the name of Jesus.

27. O Lord, raise support of mighty army of valor (Spiritual, financial, material, domestic, ministerial, numerical, mission) for me, my family, my ministry etc

locally, nationally, internationally, globally, totally in the name of Jesus.

28. O Lord, raise us up in Your glory in the name of Jesus.

29. O Lord, make way for me where there seems to be no way, in the name of Jesus

30. Father, help me not to lose my saltiness, (according to *Matthew 5:13*) in the name of Jesus.

31. O Lord, use me to wipe away the tears of people, in the name of Jesus.

32. Thank You Father for establishing the covenant of Your Glory in my life, family, ministry etc in the name of Jesus.

33. Father, take all the glory, adoration and majesty in the name of Jesus.

GRACE FOR GREATER WORKS

"I am telling you the truth: those who believe in me will do what I do; yes, they will do even greater things, because I am going to the Father." (John 14:12 GNB)

"Jesus said to them again, "Peace be with you. As the Father sent me, so I send you." Then he breathed on them and said, "Receive the Holy Spirit." (John 20:21-22 GNB)

1. Father, empower me from on high.

2. Release upon me grace for greater works in the name of Jesus.

3. Grace to do exploits, release upon us.

4. Help us to know You more in deeper dimensions for supernatural exploits.

5. Holy Ghost sit upon me for life; grant me utterances and boldness. Sit upon my calling, ministry, life, family, finances and assignment in Jesus name. I ask for divine

sitting of the Holy Spirit on me in the name of Jesus.

6. *Sing: Spirit of the Living God*
    Fall afresh on me
    Sprit of the Living God
    Fall afresh on me

7. Make us an extension of Your hand.

8. By Your grace and mercy, make us Your divine oracles like never before, and not just Your orator.

9. Lord, make us whole in the name of Jesus. Let there be total cure of all our infirmities in Jesus name.

10. We re-dedicate our children to You, visit them for unprecedented success in all their endeavors in Jesus name. Let them become symbols of Your wonders, grace, power and excellence in Jesus name.
    * You will upgrade their brains.
    * They will be better than their peers.
    * Raise them up as Your ambassadors globally.
    * Do exploits with them and for them ·
    * Release Your grace, mercy and excellence upon them.
    * Establish them in righteousness.
    * Let them reflect Your signs, wonders, goodness and nature in the name of Jesus.

11. We demand for financial and material breakthroughs, liftings, victories, empowerment, success, expansion, elevation and prosperity. Let every form of stagnation and embargo be shattered into pieces.

12. The God of my salvation arise for my help all round, in the name of Jesus.

13. Let my star bring forth "fruits": abiding, enduring, sustainable, profitable, enviable and glorious "fruits" in Jesus name. Let my "fruits" be known locally, nationally, and globally.

"Hardly a day went by without men showing up to help it wasn't long before his band seemed as large as God's own army!" (1 Chronicles 12:22 MSG)

14. Send us help as Your servants o Lord.
15. Father, give unto us the gift of men and resources; ministerially, financially, numerically, maritally, domestically, personally, in the name of Jesus.
16. Let the wealth and riches of this nation be directed to us now in the name of Jesus.
17. Doors of: wonders, miracles, signs, breakthroughs, exploits, strange acts, greater impacts, new impacts, doors of establishment, expansion, mercy, grace, glory, awesomeness, positive total change, stupendous wealth, testimonies, undeniable proofs, be opened unto us in Jesus name.

"And the key of the house of David will I lay upon his shoulder; so he shall open, and none shall shut; and he shall shut, and none shall open. " (Isaiah 22:22 KJV)

18. O Lord, be a light unto me all year round and beyond in Jesus name. Be a light unto our families, ministries, nations, careers, businesses, etc. in Jesus name.

"Do not rejoice over me, my enemy, because when I fall, I will rise; if I sit in darkness, the Lord is my light." (Micah 7:8 CEB)

19. Ask for any personal prayer of your choice.
20. Return thanks to God for answered prayers.

"CONGRATULATIONS! You are entering into your season of Harvest".

SUPERNATURAL PROVIDENCE

1. Father I thank you for all Your goodness, mercy and faithfulness over me and mine.

"So He humbled you, allowed you to hunger, and fed you with manna which you did not know nor did your fathers know, that He might make you know that man shall not live by bread alone; but man lives by every word that proceeds from the mouth of the LORD." (Deuteronomy 8:3)

2. O Lord, deliver me from every self-induced affliction, pride, and insufficiency in the name of Jesus.

"The blessing of the LORD makes one rich, And He adds no sorrow with it." Proverbs 10:22:

3. O Lord, perfect Your word and hasten to bring to pass the manifestation of my divine providence without ceasing in the name of Jesus.

2 Chronicles 15:10-15:
"So they gathered together at Jerusalem in the third month, in the fifteenth year of the reign of Asa. And they offered to the LORD at that time seven hundred bulls and seven thousand sheep from the spoil they had brought. Then they entered into a covenant to seek the LORD God of their fathers with all their heart and with all their soul; and whoever would not seek the LORD God of Israel was to be put to death, whether small or great, whether man or woman. Then they took an oath before the LORD with a loud voice, with shouting and trumpets and rams' horns. And all Judah rejoiced at the oath, for they had sworn with all their heart and sought Him with all their soul; and He was found by them, and the LORD gave them rest all around."

4. O Lord in Your mercy, grant me favour and financial rest all around in the name of Jesus.

5. O Lord, grant unto me revelation knowledge, good understanding and outstanding favours for ease and comfort in life and ministry in the name of Jesus. "You shall increase my greatness, and comfort me on every side"

6. O Lord, lift me up, make all eyes to see that You have lifted me in Jesus name.

Psalm 34:10
"The young lions lack and suffer hunger; But those who seek the LORD shall not lack any good thing".

2 Corinthians 6:10
"As sorrowful, yet always rejoicing; as poor, yet making many rich; as having nothing, and yet possessing all things."

2 Corinthians 8:9
"For you know the grace of our Lord Jesus Christ, that though He was rich, yet for your sakes He became poor, that you through His poverty might become rich."

7. O Lord the way You demonstrated supernatural providence through Jesus Christ in the midst of lack, do the same in my life, business and career in the name of Jesus.

Philippians 4:19:
"And my God shall supply all your need according to His riches in glory by Christ Jesus."

Matthew 6:8
"Therefore do not be like them. For your Father knows the

things you have need of before you ask Him."

John 16:23-24
"And in that day you will ask Me nothing. Most assuredly, I say to you, whatever you ask the Father in My name He will give you.

8. O Lord, help me to walk in ways pleasing to You and Your covenant practice for exceeding supernatural providence in the name of Jesus.

Genesis 47:27:
"So Israel dwelt in the land of Egypt, in the country of Goshen; and they had possessions there and grew and multiplied exceedingly."

Deuteronomy 8:3-4,6-7,18:
3 "So He humbled you, allowed you to hunger, and fed you with manna which you did not know nor did your fathers know, that He might make you know that man shall not live by bread alone; but man lives by every word that proceeds from the mouth of the LORD.
4 "Your garments did not wear out on you, nor did your foot swell these forty years.
6 "Therefore you shall keep the commandments of the LORD your God, to walk in His ways and to fear Him.
7 "For the LORD your God is bringing you into a good land, a land of brooks of water, of fountains and springs, that flow out of valleys and hills;
18 "And you shall remember the LORD your God, for it is He who gives you power to get wealth, that He may establish His covenant which He swore to your fathers, as it is this day."

9. O lord empower me to acquire wealth and dispense it in

a godly way in the name of Jesus.

10. O Lord empower me to be part of the answer to the questions of the sinners in the name of Jesus.

Psalm 132:15-18
"I will abundantly bless her provision; I will satisfy her poor with bread."

11. O Lord deliver me and all my interest from the heat of economic death in the name of Jesus.

Isaiah 65:24
"The wolf and the lamb shall feed together, the lion shall eat straw like the ox, and dust shall be the serpent's food. They shall not hurt nor destroy in all my holy mountain," Says the LORD.

Psalm 84:11
For the LORD God is a sun and shield; The LORD will give grace and glory; No good thing will He withhold From those who walk uprightly.

12. O Lord, show up that You are God – spiritually, financially, materially, mentally, wealth wise, need and want wise in the name of Jesus.

Genesis 8:20-22
Then Noah built an altar to the LORD, and took of every clean animal and of every clean bird, and offered burnt offerings on the altar. And the LORD smelled a soothing aroma. Then the LORD said in His heart, "I will never again curse the ground for man's sake, although the imagination of man's heart is evil from his youth; nor will I again destroy every living thing as I have done. While the earth remains, Seedtime and harvest, Cold and heat, Winter and summer, And day and night Shall

not cease.

Psalm 89:34
My covenant I will not break, Nor alter the word that has gone out of My lips.

Revelation 5:10, 12
10 And have made us kings and priests to our God; And we shall reign on the earth. "
12 saying with a loud voice: "Worthy is the Lamb who was slain To receive power and riches and wisdom, And strength and honor and glory and blessing!"

13. O Lord, empower me in Your covenant that is superior to all climates in the name of Jesus.

14. O Lord, let Your covenant practice at work in my life distinguish me as Your chosen vessel in the name of Jesus.

15. O lord, teach me and grant me access to the working knowledge of the covenant in the name of Jesus.

3 John 2
"Beloved, I pray that you may prosper in all things and be in health, just as your soul prospers."

Psalms 35:27
"Let them shout for joy and be glad, Who favor my righteous cause; And let them say continually, "Let the LORD be magnified, Who has pleasure in the prosperity of His servant."

16. O Lord, Your will for me is to prosper! Prosper me with Your supernatural providence exceeding abundantly in the name of Jesus.

Jeremiah 33:25-26
"Thus says the LORD: 'If My covenant is not with day and

night, and if I have not appointed the ordinances of heaven and earth, then I will cast away the descendants of Jacob and David My servant, so that I will not take any of his descendants to be rulers over the descendants of Abraham, Isaac, and Jacob. For I will cause their captives to return, and will have mercy on them".

Deuteronomy 8:7-10,18
7 "For the LORD your God is bringing you into a good land, a land of brooks of water, of fountains and springs, that flow out of valleys and hills;
8 "a land of wheat and barley, of vines and fig trees and pomegranates, a land of olive oil and honey;
9 "a land in which you will eat bread without scarcity, in which you will lack nothing; a land whose stones are iron and out of whose hills you can dig copper.
10 "When you have eaten and are full, then you shall bless the LORD your God for the good land which He has given you.
18 "And you shall remember the LORD your God, for it is He who gives you power to get wealth, that He may establish His covenant which He swore to your fathers, as it is this day.

17. O Lord, deliver unto me the "covenant hammer" that will break the financial hardship in my life, business and ministry in the name of Jesus.

Psalm 45:4
"And in Your majesty ride prosperously because of truth, humility, and righteousness; and Your right hand shall teach You awesome things."

Proverbs 13:15
"Good understanding gains favor, But the way of the unfaithful is hard."

Genesis 12:2-3;13:2
2 "I will make you a great nation; I will bless you And make your name great; And you shall be a blessing."
3 "I will bless those who bless you, And I will curse him who curses you; And in you all the families of the earth shall be blessed."

Genesis 13:2
"Abram was very rich in livestock, in silver, and in gold."

18. O Lord, be my never ending source! Help me to be divinely connected without ceasing in the name of Jesus.

Jeremiah 33:25-26
25 "Thus says the LORD: 'If My covenant is not with day and night, and if I have not appointed the ordinances of heaven and earth,
26 'then I will cast away the descendants of Jacob and David My servant, so that I will not take any of his descendants to be rulers over the descendants of Abraham, Isaac, and Jacob. For I will cause their captives to return, and will have mercy on them.'"

19. It is Your will for me to be rich. O Lord, enrich me for global impact in the name of Jesus.
20. O Lord, empower me with the law of productive seed time and harvest that guarantees: peace, the release of goodness, mercy and the goodies of heaven for me in the name of Jesus.

Genesis 8:22
"While the earth remains, Seedtime and harvest, Cold and heat, winter and summer, and day and night shall not cease."

Numbers 11:31
"Now a wind went out from the LORD, and it brought quail from the sea and left them fluttering near the camp, about a day's journey on this side and about a day's journey on the other side, all around the camp, and about two cubits above the surface of the ground."

2 Chronicles 9:27
"The king made silver as common in Jerusalem as stones, and he made cedar trees as abundant as the sycamores which are in the lowland."

2 Chronicles 25:9
"Then Amaziah said to the man of God, "But what shall we do about the hundred talents which I have given to the troops of Israel?" And the man of God answered, "The LORD is able to give you much more than this."

Ezra 7:28
"And has extended mercy to me before the king and his counselors, and before all the king's mighty princes. So I was encouraged, as the hand of the LORD my God was upon me; and I gathered leading men of Israel to go up with me."

21. O Lord, let money become like common stone to me; to live comfortably by reason of its abundance in the name of Jesus of Jesus.

DIVINE INCREASE

"They said to all the people of Israel, "The land we traveled through and explored is a wonderful land! And if the LORD is pleased with us, he will bring us safely into that land and give it to us. It is a rich land flowing with milk and honey. Do not rebel

against the LORD, and don't be afraid of the people of the land. They are only helpless prey to us! They have no protection, but the LORD is with us! Don't be afraid of them!" But the whole community began to talk about stoning Joshua and Caleb. Then the glorious presence of the LORD appeared to all the Israelites at the Tabernacle. And the LORD said to Moses, "How long will these people treat me with contempt? Will they never believe me, even after all the miraculous signs I have done among them? I will disown them and destroy them with a plague. Then I will make you into a nation greater and mightier than they are!" But Moses objected. "What will the Egyptians think when they hear about it?" he asked the LORD. "They know full well the power you displayed in rescuing your people from Egypt. Now if you destroy them, the Egyptians will send a report to the inhabitants of this land, who have already heard that you live among your people. They know, LORD, that you have appeared to your people face to face and that your pillar of cloud hovers over them. They know that you go before them in the pillar of cloud by day and the pillar of fire by night." (Numbers 14:7-14 NLT)

1. Father, let Your grace and mercy bring me into my wealthy place of increase in this season in the name of Jesus.
2. O Lord, forgive my trespasses, iniquities, and transgressions (known and unknown) by the blood of Jesus.
3. Father, let Your pillar of cloud and fire guide and sustain me in my wealthy place of increase in the mighty name of Jesus.

"Then he made him that remaineth have dominion over the nobles among the people: the Lord made me have dominion over

the mighty. " (Judges 5:13 KJV)

4. O Lord, empower me to have dominion over the nobles and mighty (locally, nationally, intercontinentally, globally) in the name of Jesus.

"David replied to the Philistine, "You come to me with sword, spear, and javelin, but I come to you in the name of the LORD of Heaven's Armies; the God of the armies of Israel, whom you have defied. Today the LORD will conquer you, and I will kill you and cut off your head. And then I will give the dead bodies of your men to the birds and wild animals, and the whole world will know that there is a God in Israel! And everyone assembled here will know that the LORD rescues his people, but not with sword and spear. This is the LORD's battle, and he will give you to us!" (1 Samuel 17:45-47 NLT)

5. O Lord, conquer all the forces militating against my increase (spiritually, financially, numerically materially, maritally, ministerially, economically, mentally, physically) in the name of Jesus .

6. O Lord, let the whole world know that You are the God at work in my destiny and all of my interests in the name of Jesus.

7. O Lord, show yourself mighty; rescue me from all challenges of life, ministry, business, finance, marriage, career etc in the name of Jesus.

8. O Lord, fight my battles and give me all round triumphant victories in the name of Jesus.

"Now may the LORD value my life, even as I have valued yours today. May he rescue me from all my troubles." (1 Samuel 26:24 NLT)

9. O Lord, color my life and career, and rescue me from all my troubles in the name of Jesus.

"Now go and say to my servant David, 'This is what the LORD of Heaven's Armies has declared: I took you from tending sheep in the pasture and selected you to be the leader of my people Israel. I have been with you wherever you have gone, and I have destroyed all your enemies before your eyes. Now I will make your name as famous as anyone who has ever lived on the earth! And I will provide a homeland for my people Israel, planting them in a secure place where they will never be disturbed. Evil nations won't oppress them as they've done in the past, starting from the time I appointed judges to rule my people Israel. And I will give you rest from all your enemies. "'Furthermore, the LORD declares that he will make a house for you; a dynasty of king (2 Samuel 7:8-11 NLT)

10. O Lord, speak Your increase into my life, family, business and career in the name of Jesus.
11. O Lord, make my name and career famous. Increase my greatness and comfort me on all sides in the name of Jesus.
12. O Lord, provide a homeland/estate for me (In a secured place) than what I could imagine, or think in the name of Jesus.
13. O Lord, give me rest from all my enemies in the name of Jesus.
14. O Lord, make room for me and my household ; provide a house for us in the name of Jesus. *(Psalms 127:1; 3:3)*.

"God is my strong fortress, and he makes my way perfect. He makes me as surefooted as a deer, enabling me to stand on mountain heights. He trains my hands for battle; he strengthens my arm to draw a bronze bow. You have given me your shield of

victory; your help has made me great. You have made a wide path for my feet to keep them from slipping." (2 Samuel 22:33-37 NLT)

15. O Lord, manifest Your presence in all my endeavors as my strong fortress and make my way perfect in the name of Jesus.
16. O Lord, give me Your shield of victory. Help me and make me great in the name of Jesus.
17. O Lord You have enlarged my steps under me, therefore, keep my feet from slipping in the name of Jesus.

"Do not forget the covenant I made with you, and do not worship other gods. You must worship only the LORD your God. He is the one who will rescue you from all your enemies." (2 Kings 17:38-39 NLT)

18. O Lord, help me to be faithful all the days of my life and ministry, and not to follow other gods in the name of Jesus. *(Luke 9:62)*
19. O Lord, rescue me from all my enemies in the name of Jesus.
20. O Lord, let Your joy manifest all-round strength in my life, family, career, ministry etc in the name of Jesus. *(Nehemiah 8:10)*

"Remember this good deed, O my God, and do not forget all that I have faithfully done for the Temple of my God and its services. Then I commanded the Levites to purify themselves and to guard the gates in order to preserve the holiness of the Sabbath. Remember this good deed also, O my God! Have compassion on me according to your great and unfailing love." (Nehemiah 13:14, 22 NLT)

21. O Lord, remember me in Your mercy. Reward me beyond my input in Your kingdom service in the name of Jesus. *(Hosea 10:12)*

"But the LORD watches over those who fear him, those who rely on his unfailing love. He rescues them from death and keeps them alive in times of famine." (Psalms 33:18-19 NLT)

22. O Lord, let Your fear and mercy never depart from my heart in the name of Jesus.
23. O Lord, rescue me from death; keep me alive in times of famines and all the days of my life in the name of Jesus.

God is our refuge and strength, always ready to help in times of trouble. So we will not fear when earthquakes come and the mountains crumble into the sea. Let the oceans roar and foam. Let the mountains tremble as the waters surge! Interlude (Psalm 46:1-3 NLT)

24. O God, my REFUGE and STRENGTH, my HELP in times of trouble, I thank You because You will never leave me nor forsake me in the name of Jesus.

"But the godly will flourish like palm trees and grow strong like the cedars of Lebanon. For they are transplanted to the LORD's own house. They flourish in the courts of our God. Even in old age they will still produce fruit; they will remain vital and green. They will declare, "The LORD is just! He is my rock! There is no evil in him!" (Psalms 92 :12-15 NLT)

25. O Lord, help me to flourish like a palm tree and to grow strong like the cedar of Lebanon.
26. O Lord, help me to flourish in Your court even at old

age. I will remain vital and green in the name of Jesus.

"And the LORD multiplied the people of Israel until they became too mighty for their enemies. "(Psalms 105:24 NLT)

27. O Lord, multiply us and make us more mighty for our enemies in the name of Jesus.

"The LORD brought his people out of Egypt, loaded with silver and gold; and not one among the tribes of Israel even stumbled." (Psalms 105:37 NLT)

O Lord, load us with wealth and riches in the name of Jesus.

Give Him glory for answered prayers.

Rejoice in His presence and give Him praise!

ENLARGEMENT OF COAST

"There was a man named Jabez, who was the most respected member of his family. His mother had given him the name Jabez, because his birth had been very painful. But Jabez prayed to the God of Israel, "Bless me, God, and give me much land. Be with me and keep me from anything evil that might cause me pain." And God gave him what he prayed for." (1 Chronicles 4:9-10 GNB)

1. O Lord, make me divinely more honorable in all ramifications in the name of Jesus.
2. Bless me Lord and give me more territories in the name of Jesus.
3. Be with me o Lord and keep me from anything evil that might cause me pain in the name of Jesus.
4. O Lord, grant unto me my petitions in the name of

Jesus

"Lord, I have come to you for protection; let me not be defeated! Because You are righteous, help me and rescue me. Listen to me and save me! Be my secure shelter and a strong fortress to protect me; you are my refuge and defence. My God, rescue me from the wicked, from the power of those who are cruel and evil. Sovereign Lord, I put my hope in you; I have trusted in you since I was young. I have relied on you all my life; you have protected me since the day I was born. I will always praise you. My life has been an example to many, because you have been my strong defender. (Psalms 71:1-7 GNB)

Don't stay so far away, O God; my God, hurry to my aid! May those who attack me be defeated and destroyed. May those who try to hurt me be shamed and disgraced." (Psalms 71:12-13 GNB)

You will make me greater than ever; you will comfort me again. (Psalms 71:21 GNB)

5. O Lord, protect me, never let me be defeated in all my interest in the name of Jesus.

6. O Lord, come to my aid and rescue me from the wicked in the name of Jesus.

7. O Lord, be a secured shelter and a strong fortress to protect me in the name of Jesus.

8. O Lord, you are my refuge and defense, rescue me from the power of those who are cruel and evil in the name of Jesus.

9. O Lord, make me a wonder to many globally in the name of Jesus.

10. O Lord, hurry to my aid! Show yourself strong as my strong defender in the name of Jesus.

11. O Lord, let those who attack me be destroyed. May those who try to hurt me be put to shame and be disgraced in the name of Jesus.

12. O Lord increase my greatness and comfort me on all side in the name of Jesus.

The Lord says, "I am making a new earth and new heavens. The events of the past will be completely forgotten. Be glad and rejoice for ever in what I create. The new Jerusalem I make will be full of joy, and her people will be happy. I myself will be filled with joy because of Jerusalem and her people. There will be no weeping there, no calling for help. Babies will no longer die in infancy, and all people will live out their life span. Those who live to be a hundred will be considered young. To die before that would be a sign that I had punished them. People will build houses and live in them themselves; they will not be used by someone else. They will plant vineyards and enjoy the wine; it will not be drunk by others. Like trees, my people will live long lives. They will fully enjoy the things that they have worked for.

The work they do will be successful, and their children will not meet with disaster. I will bless them and their descendants for all time to come. Even before they finish praying to me, I will answer their prayers. (Isaiah 65:17-24 GNB)

13. O Lord, establish me in Your new heaven and new earth! Let the contrary events of my life and destiny be forgotten and forgiven by Your mercy in the name of Jesus.

14. O Lord, increase my joy, gladness and laughter like never before all year round in the name of Jesus.

15. O Lord, help me to live my life span in grace, mercy, love and peace in the name of Jesus.

16. O Lord, let me build houses and let no one take them from me in the name of Jesus.

17. O Lord, as You tarry in Your coming, help me to live long enough to fulfill purpose to its fullest in the name of Jesus.

18. O Lord, grant me extravagant grace to enjoy the wine of my vineyard in the name of Jesus.

19. O Lord, help me to fully enjoy what I have worked for in the name of Jesus.

20. O Lord, help me so that I will be successful in my chosen profession in the name of Jesus.

21. O Lord, bless my children and all my descendants for all time to come. Let them not meet with disaster in the name of Jesus.

22. O Lord, establish Your covenant with us, so that before we call You will answer and while we are yet speaking, You will hear in the name of Jesus.

"The angel also showed me the river of the water of life, sparkling like crystal, and coming from the throne of God and of the Lamb and flowing down the middle of the city's street. On each side of the river was the tree of life, which bears fruit twelve times a year, once each month; and its leaves are for the healing of the nations. Nothing that is under God's curse will be found in the city. The throne of God and of the Lamb will be in the city, and his servants will worship him. They will see his face, and his name will be written on their foreheads. There shall be no more night, and they will not need lamps or sunlight, because the Lord God will be their light, and they will rule as kings for ever and ever. " (Revelation 22:1-5 GNB)

23. O Lord, bless me with the fruits You have ordained all year round for my prosperity each month without delay

in the name of Jesus.

24. O Lord, manifest the leaves for the healing of the nations all year round in my favour without ceasing in the name of Jesus.

25. O Lord, let nothing under Your curse be found in me, my family and my interests in the name of Jesus.

26. O Lord, teach me to worship You more than ever before, In the name of Jesus.

27. O Lord, let all nation see Your name on my forehead in the name of Jesus.

28. O Lord, be my everlasting light, help me to rule and reign as king forever and ever in the name of Jesus.

COVENANT OF BLESSINGS

Galatians 6:9
"And let us not grow weary while doing good, for in due season we shall reap if we do not lose heart."

Luke 8:15
"But the ones that fell on the good ground are those who, having heard the word with a noble and good heart, keep it and bear fruit with patience"

Psalms 89:34
"My covenant I will not break, nor alter the word that has gone out of my lips."

1. O Lord, help me not to be tired in my covenant walk with You in the name of Jesus.

Romans 4:20
"He did not waver at the promise of God through unbelief, but was strengthened in faith, giving glory to God"

2. O Lord, help me to wait without staggering, undaunted by negative circumstances in the name of Jesus.

Job 42:17
"So Job died, old and full of days."

Psalms 37:4, 9, 34
4 "Delight yourself also in the LORD, And He shall give you the desires of your heart.
9 For evildoers shall be cut off; But those who wait on the LORD, They shall inherit the earth.
34 Wait on the LORD, and keep His way, And He shall exalt you to inherit the land; when the wicked are cut off, you shall see it.

"Waiting on God is a man's access to great things in life"

3. O Lord, help me to wait on You for the possession of my possessions in the name of Jesus.

Philippians 4:6-7
"Be anxious for nothing, but in everything by prayer and supplication, with thanksgiving, let your requests be made known to God; and the peace of God, which surpasses all understanding, will guard your hearts and minds through Christ Jesus."

2 Peter 3:8-9
"But, beloved, do not forget this one thing, that with the Lord one day is as a thousand years, and a thousand years as one day. The Lord is not slack concerning His promise, as some count slackness, but is long suffering toward us, not willing that any should perish but that all should come to repentance."

4. O Lord, help me to live anxiety-free life in Jesus name.

"Missing God is missing good!"

5. O Lord, help me not to miss You in the name of Jesus
6. O Lord, bring about amazing and positive changes in my life with Your blessings in the name of Jesus.

Romans 10:10
"For with the heart one believes unto righteousness, and with the mouth confession is made unto salvation."

7. O Lord, help me to talk my believe without doubt in the name of Jesus.

2 Corinthians 4:13
"And since we have the same spirit of faith, according to what is written, "I believed and therefore I spoke," we also believe and therefore speak."

Romans 10:10
"For with the heart one believes unto righteousness, and with the mouth confession is made unto salvation."

8. O Lord, help me to flow effectively in all the pillars of kingdom prosperity for Your namesake.

Joshua 1:8
"This Book of the Law shall not depart from your mouth, but you shall meditate in it day and night, that you may observe to do according to all that is written in it. For then you will make your way prosperous, and then you will have good success."

9. O Lord, help me so that the book of the law must not depart from my mouth in the name of Jesus. Let me hide Your words in my heart continually.

Numbers 14:28
"Say to them, 'As I live,' says the LORD, 'just as you have

spoken in My hearing, so I will do to you"

James 3:5-6
"Even so the tongue is a little member and boasts great things. See how great a forest a little fire kindles! And the tongue is a fire, a world of iniquity. The tongue is so set among our members that it defiles the whole body, and sets on fire the course of nature; and it is set on fire by hell."

10. O Lord help me to talk, walk and manifest prosperity in the name of Jesus.
11. My tongue, I command you to be sanctified in the name of Jesus.

Proverbs 18:21
"Death and life are in the power of the tongue, and those who love it will eat its fruit."

Proverbs 13:2
"A man shall eat well by the fruit of his mouth, but the soul of the unfaithful feeds on violence."

Proverbs 18:20
"A man who has friends must himself be friendly, but there is a friend who sticks closer than a brother. Prosperity is produced on the tablet of faith, and faith is given expression through your mouth."

12. O Lord, inoculate my faith and mouth to produce results that are profitable in the name of Jesus.

Revelation 12:11
"And they overcame him by the blood of the Lamb and by the word of their testimony, and they did not love their lives to the death."

13. O Lord, help me to stop narrating trials but to start talking testimonies in the name of Jesus.
14. O Lord, empower me to enhance the speed of accomplishment in my life, business and ministry in the name of Jesus.

Psalms 35:27
"Let them shout for joy and be glad, who favor my righteous cause; And let them say continually, "Let the LORD be magnified, who has pleasure in the prosperity of His servant."

15. O Lord, grant me the grace to talk my way into the land flowing with milk and honey in the name of Jesus.

Psalms 34:12-13
"Who is the man who desires life, and loves many days, that he may see good? Keep your tongue from evil, and your lips from speaking deceit."

16. O Lord, touch my tongue with Your coal of fire in Jesus name

Mark 11:23-24
"For assuredly, I say to you, whoever says to this mountain, 'Be removed and be cast into the sea,' and does not doubt in his heart, but believes that those things he says will be done, he will have whatever he says. "Therefore I say to you, whatever things you ask when you pray, believe that you receive them, and you will have them."

17. O Lord, help me not to fail the mouth test in Jesus name.

Malachi 2:1-3
"And now, O priests, this commandment is for you. If you will

not hear, and if you will not take it to heart, to give glory to My name," Says the LORD of hosts, "I will send a curse upon you, And I will curse your blessings. Yes, I have cursed them already, because you do not take it to heart."

Isaiah 51:1-2

"1 "Listen to me, you who follow after righteousness, you who seek the LORD: Look to the rock from which you were hewn, And to the hole of the pit from which you were dug. Look to Abraham your father, And to Sarah who bore you; For I called him alone, And blessed him and increased him."

Romans 4:18-20

"Who, contrary to hope, in hope believed, so that he became the father of many nations, according to what was spoken, "So shall your descendants be. And not being weak in faith, he did not consider his own body, already dead (since he was about a hundred years old), and the deadness of Sarah's womb. He did not waver at the promise of God through unbelief, but was strengthened in faith, giving glory to God"

18. O Lord, help me to give unto You quality seed and glory always in the name of Jesus.

Psalms 67:5-7

"Let the peoples praise You, O God; Let all the peoples praise you. Then the earth shall yield her increase; God, our own God, shall bless us. God shall bless us, and all the ends of the earth shall fear Him."

19. O Lord ,cause me to be thankful without ceasing in the name of Jesus.

Hebrews 12:1-2

"Therefore we also, since we are surrounded by so great a cloud

of witnesses, let us lay aside every weight, and the sin which so easily ensnares us, and let us run with endurance the race that is set before us, looking unto Jesus, the author and finisher of our faith, who for the joy that was set before Him endured the cross, despising the shame, and has sat down at the right hand of the throne of God."

Psalms 121:1-3
"I will lift up my eyes to the hills-From whence comes my help? My help comes from the LORD, Who made heaven and earth. He will not allow your foot to be moved; He who keeps you will not slumber."

20. O Lord, help me to stop seeing shadows but to completely focus on You in the name of Jesus.

"Talking and thanking God is the watering dimension in the school of prosperity."

21. O Lord, help me to be effective in talking and thanking You always, in Jesus name.
22. O Lord, deliver me from walking with murmurers and unproductive friends in the name of Jesus.
23. O Lord, I ask for grace to live a life of thanksgiving and to remain thankful no matter the situation and circumstance. I receive it right now in the name of Jesus.
24. I decree my business and career will never go down in the name of Jesus.

Everything that accompanies the covenant of giving becomes my portion in the name of Jesus.

I will never be trapped in borrowing again in the name of Jesus.

For every work I have done, I will be paid in the name of Jesus.

No evil will cheat me of my labour anymore in the name of Jesus.

This day marks the end of all my struggles in the name of Jesus.

* I am blessed!
* I am fruitful!!
* I am prosperous!!!

FINANCIAL PROSPERITY

3 John 2:
" Beloved, I pray that you may prosper in all things and be in health, just as your soul prospers" (NKJV)

1. Father, thank You for prospering me exceedingly in the name of Jesus.
2. Prosperity is a state of no Lack; Father, prosper me exceeding mightily in the name of Jesus.

2 Chronicles 9:27
"The king made silver as common in Jerusalem as stones, and he made cedar trees as abundant as the sycamores which are in the lowland" (NKJV)

2 Chronicles 25:9b
"But what shall we do about the hundred talents which I have given to the troops of Israel?"(NKJV)

3. Father, thank You for honoring me with bountiful harvest.

2 Corinthians 9:6-12
"But this I say: He who sows sparingly will also reap sparingly, and he who sows bountifully will also reap bountifully. So let each one give as he purposes in his heart, not grudgingly or of necessity; for God loves a cheerful giver. And God is able to make all grace abound toward you, that you, always having all sufficiency in all things, may have an abundance for every good work. As it is written: He has dispersed abroad, He has given to the poor; His righteousness endures forever."

Now may He who supplies seed to the sower, and bread for food, supply and multiply the seed you have sown and increase the fruits of your righteousness, while you are enriched in everything for all liberality, which causes thanksgiving through us to God. For the administration of this service not only supplies the needs of the saints, but also is abounding through many thanksgivings to God"(NKJV).

2 Corinthians 8:9
"For you know the grace of our Lord Jesus Christ, that though He was rich, yet for your sakes He became poor, that you through His poverty might become rich(NKJV)

4. Every giver provokes divine blessings; Father, let my giving invoke Your divine blessings without ceasing, in the name of Jesus

Deuteronomy 29:29
"The secret things belong to the Lord our God, but those things which are revealed belong to us and to our children forever, that we may do all the words of this law. NKJV

Psalm 25:13-15
"He himself shall dwell in prosperity, And his descendants

shall inherit the earth. The secret of the Lord is with those who fear Him, And He will show them His covenant. My eyes are ever toward the Lord, For He shall pluck my feet out of the net."(NKJV)

5. Whatever might have been tying me down from enjoying the beauties of God in life, Lord, reveal them to me now in the name of Jesus.

1 Corinthians 16:9
For a great and effective door has opened to me, and there are many adversaries".(NKJV)

Mark 11:1-5
"Now when they drew near Jerusalem, to Bethphage and Bethany, at the Mount of Olives, He sent two of His disciples; and He said to them, "Go into the village opposite you; and as soon as you have entered it you will find a colt tied, on which no one has sat. Loose it and bring it. And if anyone says to you, 'Why are you doing this?' say, 'The Lord has need of it,' and immediately he will send it here." So they went their way, and found the colt tied by the door outside on the street, and they loosed it "(NKJV)

6. Every tied down issues of my life, my family, my career, my business, be released now in the name of Jesus.

Job 42:2
"I know that You can do everything, And that no purpose of Yours can be withheld from You.(NKJV)

7. O Lord, pick me out of poverty today and throw me into the realms of prosperity in the name of Jesus.

Genesis. 12:1-4

"Get out of your country, From your family, And from your father's house, To a land that I will show you. I will make you a great nation; I will bless you, And make your name great; And you shall be a blessing. I will bless those who bless you, And I will curse him who curses you; And in you all the families of the earth shall be blessed." So Abram departed as the Lord had spoken to him, and Lot went with him. And Abram was seventy-five years old when he departed from Haran." (NKJV)

8. Father, enable me to be a blessing to my generation in Jesus name.

Psalms 1:1-3

"Blessed is the man, Who walks not in the counsel of the ungodly, Nor stands in the path of sinners, Nor sits in the seat of the scornful; But his delight is in the law of the Lord, And in His law he meditates day and night. He shall be like a tree Planted by the rivers of water, That brings forth its fruit in its season, Whose leaf also shall not wither; And whatever he does shall prosper." (NKJV)

3 John 2

" Beloved, I pray that you may prosper in all things and be in health, just as your soul prospers" (NKJV)

Philipians 4:19

And my God shall supply all your need according to His riches in glory by Christ Jesus (NKJV)

9. Lord Jesus, I turn to You as my source, prosper me exceedingly in Jesus name.

John 4:48

"Then Jesus said to him, "Unless you people see signs and

wonders, you will by no means believe." (NKJV)

Isaiah 60:1-3
"Arise, shine; For your light has come! And the glory of the Lord is risen upon you. For behold, the darkness shall cover the earth, And deep darkness the people; But the Lord will arise over you, And His glory will be seen upon you. The Gentiles shall come to your light, And kings to the brightness of your rising. "(NKJV)

Acts 2:22
"Men of Israel, hear these words: Jesus of Nazareth, a Man attested by God to you by miracles, wonders, and signs which God did through Him in your midst, as you yourselves also know(NKJV).

10. Father, help me to locate Your word on prosperity and act on it for mighty works of prosperity in the name of Jesus.

Haggai 2:6-8
"For thus says the Lord of hosts:'Once more (it is a little while) I will shake heaven and earth, the sea and dry land; and I will shake all nations, and they shall come to the Desire of All Nations, and I will fill this temple with glory,' says the Lord of hosts. 'The silver is Mine, and the gold is Mine,' says the Lord of hosts.(NKJV)

Zechariah 1:17
"Again proclaim, saying, 'Thus says the Lord of hosts:"My cities shall again spread out through prosperity; The Lord will again comfort Zion, And will again choose Jerusalem."
(NKJV)

Matt 24:14
And this gospel of the kingdom will be preached in all the world as a witness to all the nations, and then the end will come. (NKJV)

11. O Lord, use me to prosper Your kingdom In the name of Jesus.

Psalms 25:14
"The secret of the Lord is with those who fear Him, And He will show them His covenant. "(NKJV)

Psalms 89:34
"My covenant I will not break, Nor alter the word that has gone out of My lips."(NKJV)

Jeremiah 33:20-21
"Thus says the Lord: 'If you can break My covenant with the day and My covenant with the night, so that there will not be day and night in their season, then My covenant may also be broken with David My servant, so that he shall not have a son to reign on his throne, and with the Levites, the priests, My ministers."(NKJV)

Jeremiah 33:25-26
"Thus says the Lord: 'If My covenant is not with day and night, and if I have not appointed the ordinances of heaven and earth, then I will cast away the descendants of Jacob and David My servant, so that I will not take any of his descendants to be rulers over the descendants of Abraham, Isaac, and Jacob. For I will cause their captives to return, and will have mercy on them." (NKJV)

12. O Lord, show me the covenant secrets that will make things to blossom in my life, in the name of Jesus.

13. Since abundance is my heritage, O Lord, help me to align with Your covenant of prosperity in the name of Jesus.

Psalm 119:130
"The entrance of Your words gives light; It gives understanding to the simple." (NKJV)

Galatians 3:13-14
"Christ has redeemed us from the curse of the law, having become a curse for us (for it is written, "Cursed is everyone who hangs on a tree"), that the blessing of Abraham might come upon the Gentiles in Christ Jesus, that we might receive the promise of the Spirit through faith." (NKJV)

14. I curse every hold of poverty in my life, in the precious name of Jesus!

Ephesians 1:18
"the eyes of your understanding being enlightened; that you may know what is the hope of His calling, what are the riches of the glory of His inheritance in the saints". (NKJV)

15. O Lord, let the eyes of my understanding be enlightened for a better life in the name of Jesus.

Psalms 103:7
"He made known His ways to Moses, His acts to the children of Israel." (NKJV)

Psalms 32:8
"I will instruct you and teach you in the way you should go; I will guide you with My eye." (NKJV)

Deuteronomy 29:29
"The secret things belong to the Lord our God, but those things

which are revealed belong to us and to our children forever, that we may do all the words of this law. " (NKJV)

16. Teach Me Lord, how to make it without ceasing in the name of Jesus.

2 Corinthians 8:9
"For you know the grace of our Lord Jesus Christ, that though He was rich, yet for your sakes He became poor, that you through His poverty might become rich "(NKJV)

17. I decree that poverty be swallowed up in victory, in our children, ministries, church, life, family, business, destiny, and nation in the name of Jesus.

Psalm 1:3
"He shall be like a tree, planted by the rivers of water, That brings forth its fruit in its season, Whose leaf also shall not wither; And whatever he does shall prosper. "(NKJV)

Genesis 26:1-3
"There was a famine in the land, besides the first famine that was in the days of Abraham. And Isaac went to Abimelech king of the Philistines, in Gerar. Then the Lord appeared to him and said:"Do not go down to Egypt; live in the land of which I shall tell you." (NKJV)

Genesis 26:12-16
"Then Isaac sowed in that land, and reaped in the same year a hundredfold; and the Lord blessed him. 13 The man began to prosper, and continued prospering until he became very prosperous; 14 for he had possessions of flocks and possessions of herds and a great number of servants. So the Philistines envied him. 15 Now the Philistines had stopped up all the wells which his father's servants had dug in the days of Abraham his

father, and they had filled them with earth. 16 And Abimelech said to Isaac, "Go away from us, for you are much mightier than we." (NKJV)

18. O Lord, work a work of prosperity in our churches for Your people to flourish and Your kingdom to progress. Let amazing things be happening in Your church in the name of Jesus.

Revelation 5:12
"Saying with a loud voice:"Worthy is the Lamb who was slain To receive power and riches and wisdom, And strength and honor and glory and blessing!" (NKJV)

Romans 10:12
"For there is no distinction between Jew and Greek, for the same Lord over all is rich to all who call upon Him." (NKJV)

Galatians 3:13-14
"Christ has redeemed us from the curse of the law, having become a curse for us (for it is written, "Cursed is everyone who hangs on a tree"), 14 that the blessing of Abraham might come upon the Gentiles in Christ Jesus, that we might receive the promise of the Spirit through faith." (NKJV)

19. Lord, You redeemed me to be rich. Help me not to abuse my redemption for Your name sake.

Matt 25:34-40
"Then the King will say to those on His right hand, 'Come, you blessed of My Father, inherit the kingdom prepared for you from the foundation of the world: for I was hungry and you gave Me food; I was thirsty and you gave Me drink; I was a stranger and you took Me in; I was naked and you clothed Me; I was sick and you visited Me; I was in prison and you came to

Me.' "Then the righteous will answer Him, saying, 'Lord, when did we see You hungry and feed You, or thirsty and give You drink? When did we see You a stranger and take You in, or naked and clothe You? Or when did we see You sick, or in prison, and come to You?' And the King will answer and say to them, 'Assuredly, I say to you, inasmuch as you did it to one of the least of these My brethren, you did it to Me." (NKJV)

20. Wealth is my heritage! Abundance is my birth right!! I am saved to display Your wealth!!! Manifest it now, in the name of Jesus.

1 Corinthians 3:21.
"Therefore let no one boast in men. For all things are yours."

Joel 3:10.
"Beat your plowshares into swords And your pruning hooks into spears; Let the weak say, 'I am strong.

21. Since poverty-mentality is satanic slavery, I decree I am free from it, in the name of Jesus.

Ephesians 1:8.
"knowing that whatever good anyone does, he will receive the same from the Lord, whether he is a slave or free."

Psalm 25:12-15.
"Who is the man that fears the LORD? Him shall He teach in the way He chooses. He himself shall dwell in prosperity, And his descendants shall inherit the earth. The secret of the LORD is with those who fear Him, And He will show them His covenant. My eyes are ever toward the LORD, For He shall pluck my feet out of the net.

Deuteronomy 29:29.
The secret things belong to the LORD our God, but those things which are revealed belong to us and to our children forever, that we may do all the words of this law."

22. O Lord, promise me supernatural access into Your secrets concerning Kingdom Prosperity in Jesus name.

2 Chronicles 9:27.
"The king made silver as common in Jerusalem as stones, and he made cedar trees as abundant as the sycamores which are in the lowland."

Ezra 7:28.
"And has extended mercy to me before the king and his counselors, and before all the king's mighty princes. So I was encouraged, as the hand of the LORD my God was upon me; and I gathered leading men of Israel to go up with me."

Zechariah 1:17.
"Again proclaim, saying, 'Thus says the LORD of hosts: " My cities shall again spread out through prosperity; The LORD will again comfort Zion, And will again choose Jerusalem".

23. I decree from henceforth, money will respect me in the name of Jesus.
24. O Lord, establish me in Your state of light and prosperity in the name of Jesus.

Isaiah 60:1-2
"Arise, shine; For your light has come! And the glory of the LORD is risen upon you. For behold, the darkness shall cover the earth, And deep darkness the people; But the LORD will arise over you, And His glory will be seen upon you."

Psalm5:12.
"For You, O LORD, will bless the righteous; With favor You will surround him as with a shield."

Psalm102:13,16
"You will arise and have mercy on Zion; For the time to favor her, Yes, the set time, has come. For the LORD shall build up Zion; He shall appear in His glory."

25. Let this day mark the breaking forth of heaven's light and favour in my life, in the name of Jesus.

Psalm 119:105
"Your word is a lamp to my feet And a light to my path.

Numbers 11:31
Now a wind went out from the LORD, and it brought quail from the sea and left them fluttering near the camp, about a day's journey on this side and about a day's journey on the other side, all around the camp, and about two cubits above the surface of the ground."

26. O lord, let me experience Your touch in a new way for supernatural exploits in the name of Jesus.

3 John 2
"Beloved, I pray that you may prosper in all things and be in health, just as your soul prospers."NKJV

27. O Lord, lead me to find a better state of well-being with Your covenant of abundance in the name of Jesus.

Psalm23:1-2
"The LORD is my shepherd; I shall not want. He makes me to lie down in green pastures; He leads me beside the still waters. "

28. O Lord grant me a way of escape from every discomfort of life in Jesus name.

Haggai 2:19
"Is the seed still in the barn? As yet the vine, the fig tree, the pomegranate, and the olive tree have not yielded fruit. But from this day I will bless you."

Proverbs 14:23
"In all labor there is profit, But idle chatter leads only to poverty."

Proverbs 23:18
"For surely there is a hereafter, And your hope will not be cut off."

Proverbs 24:14
"So shall the knowledge of wisdom be to your soul; If you have found it, there is a prospect, And your hope will not be cut off."

29. O Lord, put an end to all my struggle this day in the name of Jesus.

Zechariah 1:17
"Again proclaim, saying, 'Thus says the LORD of hosts: " My cities shall again spread out through prosperity; The LORD will again comfort Zion, And will again choose Jerusalem."

Ephesians 4:28
"Let him who stole steal no longer, but rather let him labor, working with his hands what is good, that he may have something to give him who has need."

3 John 2
"The Elder, To the beloved Gaius, whom I love in truth"

Luke 6:28
"bless those who curse you, and pray for those who spitefully use you."

30. O Lord, my source -I declare that; This is my day of prosperity, and I receive it through Your word.
    * I am set to be a covenant practitioner.
    * I will not live in lack and poverty.
    * I am blessed.
    * I am fruitful.
    * I am prosperous.
    * I am a great nation.
    * I am a blessing to my generation.
    * Lord, I'm tired of looking elsewhere.
    * I look not at men anymore.
    * I am looking up to you.
    * Help me O Lord! in Jesus name.

Philipians 4:15
"Now you Philippians know also that in the beginning of the gospel, when I departed from Macedonia, no church shared with me concerning giving and receiving but you only."NKJV

Philipians 4:19
"And my God shall supply all your need according to His riches in glory by Christ Jesus."NKJV

Deuteronomy 8:18
"And you shall remember the Lord your God, for it is He who gives you power to get wealth, that He may establish His covenant which He swore to your fathers, as it is this day."NKJV

Hebrews 7:7-8
"Now beyond all contradiction the lesser is blessed by the better. 8 Here mortal men receive tithes, but there he receives them, of whom it is witnessed that he lives."NKJV

Galatians 6:7-8
"Do not be deceived, God is not mocked; for whatever a man sows, that he will also reap."NKJV

2 Corinthians 9:10
"Now may He who supplies seed to the sower, and bread for food, supply and multiply the seed you have sown and increase the fruits of your righteousness."NKJV

Matthew 17:20
"So Jesus said to them, "Because of your unbelief; for assuredly, I say to you, if you have faith as a mustard seed, you will say to this mountain, 'Move from here to there,' and it will move; and nothing will be impossible for you."NKJV

Acts 20:35
"I have shown you in every way, by laboring like this, that you must support the weak. And remember the words of the Lord Jesus, that He said, 'It is more blessed to give than to receive."(NKJV)

2 Corinthians 9:7-8
"So let each one give as he purposes in his heart, not grudgingly or of necessity; for God loves a cheerful giver."(NKJV)

Hebrews 6:14
"Saying, "Surely blessing I will bless you, and multiplying I will multiply you."(NKJV)

31. Since the power for wealth is released on the platform of

covenant, O Lord, I step into the covenant. Let me encounter the power to get wealth.

Psalms 89:34
"My covenant I will not break, Nor alter the word that has gone out of My lips."(NKJV)

Jeremiah 33:20-21
"Thus says the Lord: 'If you can break My covenant with the day and My covenant with the night, so that there will not be day and night in their season, 21 then My covenant may also be broken with David My servant, so that he shall not have a son to reign on his throne, and with the Levites, the priests, My ministers."(NKJV)

Jeremiah 33:25-26
"Thus says the Lord: 'If My covenant is not with day and night, and if I have not appointed the ordinances of heaven and earth, 26 then I will cast away the descendants of Jacob and David My servant, so that I will not take any of his descendants to be rulers over the descendants of Abraham, Isaac, and Jacob. For I will cause their captives to return, and will have mercy on them." (NKJV)

2 Chronicles 15:12-13
"Then they entered into a covenant to seek the Lord God of their fathers with all their heart and with all their soul"

2 Chronicles 15:15
"And all Judah rejoiced at the oath, for they had sworn with all their heart and sought Him with all their soul; and He was found by them, and the Lord gave them rest all around."NKJV

Genesis 8:22
"While the earth remains, Seedtime and harvest, Cold and heat, Winter and summer, And day and night Shall not cease."(NKJV)

32. Father, let the covenant practices bring proofs into my life, business and ministry in the name of Jesus. (Remember that harvest only answers to seed time)

Genesis 12:1-2
"Get out of your country, From your family, And from your father's house, To a land that I will show you.
I will make you a great nation; I will bless you, And make your name great; And you shall be a blessing."(NKJV)

Genesis 12:9-11
"So Abram journeyed, going on still toward the South. Now there was a famine in the land, and Abram went down to Egypt to dwell there, for the famine was severe in the land."(NKJV)

Genesis 13:2
"Abram was very rich in livestock, in silver, and in gold."
(NKJV)

Genesis 26:1
"There was a famine in the land, besides the first famine that was in the days of Abraham. And Isaac went to Abimelech king of the Philistines, in Gerar."(NKJV)

Genesis 26:12
"Then Isaac sowed in that land, and reaped in the same year a hundredfold; and the Lord blessed him."(NKJV)

Genesis 12:13-14
"Please say you are my sister, that it may be well with me for

your sake, and that I may live because of you." So it was, when Abram came into Egypt, that the Egyptians saw the woman, that she was very beautiful." (NKJV)

Genesis 43:1
"Now the famine was severe in the land." (NKJV)

33. O Lord, let Your covenant prevail in my destiny in the name of Jesus.

Psalm 37:18
"The Lord knows the days of the upright, And their inheritance shall be forever." (NKJV)

Proverbs 10:22
"The blessing of the Lord makes one rich, And He adds no sorrow with it." NKJV

34. I decree, I will never lose control anymore in my life in the name of Jesus.

Psalm 121:1
"I will lift up my eyes to the hills; From whence comes my help?" (NKJV)

Psalm 60:1
"O God, You have cast us off; You have broken us down; You have been displeased; Oh, restore us again!" (NKJV)

Isa 60:3
"The Gentiles shall come to your light, And kings to the brightness of your rising." (NKJV)

Genesis 47:13
"Now there was no bread in all the land; for the famine was very severe, so that the land of Egypt and the land of Canaan

languished because of the famine. " (NKJV)

Genesis 47:15
"So when the money failed in the land of Egypt and in the land of Canaan, all the Egyptians came to Joseph and said, "Give us bread, for why should we die in your presence? For the money has failed." (NKJV)

Genesis 47:18
"When that year had ended, they came to him the next year and said to him, "We will not hide from my lord that our money is gone; my lord also has our herds of livestock. There is nothing left in the sight of my lord but our bodies and our lands." (NKJV)

Genesis 47:27
"So Israel dwelt in the land of Egypt, in the country of Goshen; and they had possessions there and grew and multiplied exceedingly." (NKJV)

35. O Lord, let my hope be built in You and in the precious blood of Jesus.
36. Father, I receive extravagant grace to be a covenant keeper and great achiever in the name of Jesus.

Ephesians 6:10-11
"Finally, my brethren, be strong in the Lord and in the power of His might. "(NKJV)

Joshua 1:3
"Every place that the sole of your foot will tread upon I have given you, as I said to Moses. "(NKJV)

Joshua 1:6-9
"Be strong and of good courage, for to this people you shall

divide as an inheritance the land which I swore to their fathers to give them. Only be strong and very courageous, that you may observe to do according to all the law which Moses My servant commanded you; do not turn from it to the right hand or to the left, that you may prosper wherever you go. This Book of the Law shall not depart from your mouth, but you shall meditate in it day and night, that you may observe to do according to all that is written in it. For then you will make your way prosperous, and then you will have good success. Have I not commanded you? Be strong and of good courage; do not be afraid, nor be dismayed, for the Lord your God is with you wherever you go. "(NKJV)

37. Lord, help me to stand strong under Your covenant and Your covering all the days of my life as a life style in the name of Jesus.

Matthew 18:18
"Assuredly, I say to you, whatever you bind on earth will be bound in heaven, and whatever you loose on earth will be loosed in heaven. "(NKJV)

38. Let everything that is against me bow to the power of this covenant, in the mighty name of Jesus.

Psalm 11:3
"If the foundations are destroyed, What can the righteous do?"(NKJV)

Isaiah 3:10
"Say to the righteous that it shall be well with them, For they shall eat the fruit of their doings. " (NKJV)

Psalms 102:16
"For the Lord shall build up Zion; He shall appear in His

glory."(NKJV)

Isaiah 2:2
"Now it shall come to pass in the latter days, That the mountain of the Lord's house Shall be established on the top of the mountains, And shall be exalted above the hills; And all nations shall flow to it." (NKJV)

2 Timothy 2:19
"Nevertheless the solid foundation of God stands, having this seal: "The Lord knows those who are His," and, "Let everyone who names the name of Christ depart from iniquity."(NKJV)

2 Timothy 3:16
"All Scripture is given by inspiration of God, and is profitable for doctrine, for reproof, for correction, for instruction in righteousness" (NKJV)

Genesis 3:9-10
Then the Lord God called to Adam and said to him, "Where are you?" , So he said, "I heard Your voice in the garden, and I was afraid because I was naked; and I hid myself." (NKJV)

Genesis 2:15-17
Then the Lord God took the man and put him in the garden of Eden to tend and keep it. 16 And the Lord God commanded the man, saying, "Of every tree of the garden you may freely eat; 17 but of the tree of the knowledge of good and evil you shall not eat, for in the day that you eat of it you shall surely die." (NKJV)

Genesis 3:6-7
So when the woman saw that the tree was good for food, that it was pleasant to the eyes, and a tree desirable to make one wise,

she took of its fruit and ate. She also gave to her husband with her, and he ate. 7 Then the eyes of both of them were opened, and they knew that they were naked; and they sewed fig leaves together and made themselves coverings. NKJV

Genesis 3:23-24
therefore the Lord God sent him out of the garden of Eden to till the ground from which he was taken. 24 So He drove out the man; and He placed cherubim at the east of the garden of Eden, and a flaming sword which turned every way, to guard the way to the tree of life.(NKJV)

39. O Lord, help rebuild my foundation for prosperity in the name of Jesus

Psalms 66:18
"If I regard iniquity in my heart, The Lord will not hear." (NKJV)

2 Timothy 2:19
Nevertheless the solid foundation of God stands, having this seal: "The Lord knows those who are His," and, "Let everyone who names the name of Christ depart from iniquity." (NKJV)

Job 22:23-24
If you return to the Almighty, you will be built up; You will remove iniquity far from your tents. Then you will lay your gold in the dust, And the gold of Ophir among the stones of the brooks.(NKJV)

40. You appetite for sin, I come against you with the blood of Jesus.

GOD YOU ARE MY SOURCE

1 Corinthians 2:14
But the natural man does not receive the things of the Spirit of God, for they are foolishness to him; nor can he know them, because they are spiritually discerned.

Rev. 22:15
But outside are dogs and sorcerers and sexually immoral and murderers and idolaters, and whoever loves and practices a lie.

Mark 4:11
And He said to them, "To you it has been given to know the mystery of the kingdom of God; but to those who are outside, all things come in parables.

2 Peter 2:20,22
For if, after they have escaped the pollutions of the world through the knowledge of the Lord and Savior Jesus Christ, they are again entangled in them and overcome, the latter end is worse for them than the beginning. But it has happened to them according to the true proverb: "A dog returns to his own vomit," and, "a sow, having washed, to her wallowing in the mire."

Psalm 25:12
Who is the man that fears the LORD? Him shall He teach in the way He chooses. The secret of the LORD is with those who fear Him, And He will show them His covenant

Job 1:1
There was a man in the land of Uz, whose name was Job; and that man was blameless and upright, and one who feared God and shunned evil. Since the fear of God is what qualifies one for access into the secrets of God

1. O Lord! let me shine with Your secrets for financial and natural exploits in the name of Jesus.

Psalm60:11
Give us help from trouble, For the help of man is useless.

Proverbs 1:7
The fear of the LORD is the beginning of knowledge, But fools despise wisdom and instruction.

Psalm 1:3
Blessed is the man Who walks not in the counsel of the ungodly, Nor stands in the path of sinners, Nor sits in the seat of the scornful; But his delight is in the law of the LORD, And in His law he meditates day and night. He shall be like a tree Planted by the rivers of water, That brings forth its fruit in its season, Whose leaf also shall not wither; And whatever he does shall prosper.

2. Help me o Lord. Let every household wickedness of my life be destroyed in Jesus name

Hebrews 11:24-34
By faith Moses, when he became of age, refused to be called the son of Pharaoh's daughter, Choosing rather to suffer affliction with the people of God than to enjoy the passing pleasures of sin, Esteeming the reproach of Christ greater riches than the treasures in Egypt; for he looked to the reward. By faith he forsook Egypt, not fearing the wrath of the king; for he endured as seeing Him who is invisible. By faith he kept the Passover and the sprinkling of blood, lest he who destroyed the firstborn should touch them. By faith they passed through the Red Sea as by dry land, whereas the Egyptians, attempting to do so, were drowned. By faith the walls of Jericho fell down after they were

encircled for seven days. By faith the harlot Rahab did not perish with those who did not believe, when she had received the spies with peace. And what more shall I say? For the time would fail me to tell of Gideon and Barak and Samson and Jephthah, also of David and Samuel and the prophets: who through faith subdued kingdoms, worked righteousness, obtained promises, stopped the mouths of lions, Quenched the violence of fire, escaped the edge of the sword, out of weakness were made strong, became valiant in battle, turned to flight the armies of the aliens.

Psalm 16:11
You will show me the path of life; In Your presence is fullness of joy; At Your right hand are pleasures forevermore

3. O Lord, grant the enabling environment of Eden - where there is no lack or want, place of plenty, where favour flows freely, in the name of Jesus

Hosea 14:2
Take words with you, And return to the LORD. Say to Him, "Take away all iniquity; Receive us graciously, For we will offer the sacrifices of our lips.

Job 22:21-25
"Now acquaint yourself with Him, and be at peace; Thereby good will come to you. Receive, please, instruction from His mouth, And lay up His words in your heart. If you return to the Almighty, you will be built up; You will remove iniquity far from your tents. Then you will lay your gold in the dust, And the gold of Ophir among the stones of the brooks. Yes, the Almighty will be your gold And your precious silver;

4. O Lord, help me to respond positively to every word of

Your mouth in the name of Jesus.

3 John 2
Beloved, I pray that you may prosper in all things and be in health, just as your soul prospers.

Isaiah 51:3
For the LORD will comfort Zion, He will comfort all her waste places; He will make her wilderness like Eden, And her desert like the garden of the LORD; Joy and gladness will be found in it, Thanksgiving and the voice of melody.

5.   I will not know the meaning of lack anymore in life, in the name of Jesus.

2 Chronicles 15:12
Then they entered into a covenant to seek the LORD God of their fathers with all their heart and with all their soul; And all Judah rejoiced at the oath, for they had sworn with all their heart and sought Him with all their soul; and He was found by them, and the LORD gave them rest all around.

Psalm 92:12
The righteous shall flourish like a palm tree, He shall grow like a cedar in Lebanon. Those who are planted in the house of the LORD Shall flourish in the courts of our God. They shall still bear fruit in old age; They shall be fresh and flourishing, To declare that the LORD is upright; He is my rock, and there is no unrighteousness in Him.

6.   O Lord, keep my feet in your house, in the name of Jesus

7.   I command blessing in my coming in and my going out! I command blessing over my store house and my baskets. I command the rain of heaven over the works

of my hands, in the name of Jesus.

Proverbs 3:13-16
Happy is the man who finds wisdom, And the man who gains understanding; For her proceeds are better than the profits of silver, And her gain than fine gold. She is more precious than rubies, And all the things you may desire cannot compare with her. Length of days is in her right hand, In her left hand riches and honor

8.   O Lord, help me to consecrate myself in holiness and purity in the name of Jesus.

Proverbs 13:11
Wealth gained by dishonesty will be diminished, But he who gathers by labor will increase.

Ezekiel 36:33
Thus says the Lord GOD: "On the day that I cleanse you from all your iniquities, I will also enable you to dwell in the cities, and the ruins shall be rebuilt.

Genesis 17:1
When Abram was ninety-nine years old, the LORD appeared to Abram and said to him, "I am Almighty God; walk before Me and be blameless.

Genesis 5:24
And Enoch walked with God; and he was not, for God took him.

Hebrews 11:5
By faith Enoch was taken away so that he did not see death, "and was not found, because God had taken him"; for before he was taken he had this testimony, that he pleased God.

9. As I receive grace for consecration, O Lord give my life colour and bring me back to the garden of comfort in the name of Jesus.

Psalm 110:3
Your people shall be volunteers In the day of Your power; In the beauties of holiness, from the womb of the morning, You have the dew of Your youth.

Proverbs 11:3
The integrity of the upright will guide them, But the perversity of the unfaithful will destroy them.

Psalm 112:2
His descendants will be mighty on earth; The generation of the upright will be blessed.

Psalm 92:12
The righteous shall flourish like a palm tree, He shall grow like a cedar in Lebanon.

2 Timothy 2:19-21
Nevertheless the solid foundation of God stands, having this seal: "The Lord knows those who are His," and, "Let everyone who names the name of Christ depart from iniquity." But in a great house there are not only vessels of gold and silver, but also of wood and clay, some for honor and some for dishonor. Therefore if anyone cleanses himself from the latter, he will be a vessel for honor, sanctified and useful for the Master, prepared for every good work.

Proverbs 1:32
For the turning away of the simple will slay them, And the complacency of fools will destroy them.

Proverbs 14:9
Fools mock at sin, But among the upright there is favor.

10. O Lord, help me to live straight in the name of Jesus
11. Father, help me to put my heart in line with You, and my habit under covenant control in the name of Jesus.

Hosea 14:2
Take words with you, And return to the LORD. Say to Him, "Take away all iniquity; Receive us graciously, For we will offer the sacrifices of our lips.

Job 22:21-25
"Now acquaint yourself with Him, and be at peace; Thereby good will come to you. Receive, please, instruction from His mouth, And lay up His words in your heart. If you return to the Almighty, you will be built up; You will remove iniquity far from your tents. Then you will lay your gold in the dust, And the gold of Ophir among the stones of the brooks. Yes, the Almighty will be your gold And your precious silver.

12. O Lord, help me not to harbour unrighteousness in my heart in the name of Jesus.

Malachi 3:7
Yet from the days of your fathers, You have gone away from My ordinances, And have not kept them. Return to Me, and I will return to you, "Says the Lord of hosts. "But you said, 'In what way shall we return? NKJV

Job 22:23-25
If you return to the Almighty, you will be built up; You will remove iniquity far from your tents. Then you will lay your gold in the dust, And the gold of Ophir among the stones of the

brooks. Yes, the Almighty will be your gold ,And your precious silver NKJV.

Proverbs 23:26
My son, give me your heart, And let your eyes observe my ways. NKJV

2 Chronicles 26:9
And Uzziah built towers in Jerusalem at the Corner Gate, at the Valley Gate, and at the corner buttress of the wall; then he fortified them. NKJV.

Psalm 112:1-3
Praise the Lord, blessed is the man who fears the Lord, Who delights greatly in His commandments. His descendants will be mighty on earth; The generation of the upright will be blessed. Wealth and riches will be in his house. NKJV

Genesis 41:38-45
And Pharaoh said to his servants, "Can we find such a one as this, a man in whom is the Spirit of God?" Then Pharaoh said to Joseph, "Inasmuch as God has shown you all this, there is no one as discerning and wise as you. You shall be over my house, and all my people shall be ruled according to your word; only in regard to the throne will I be greater than you." And Pharaoh said to Joseph, "See, I have set you over all the land of Egypt." Then Pharaoh took his signet ring off his hand and put it on Joseph's hand; and he clothed him in garments of fine linen and put a gold chain around his neck. And he had him ride in the second chariot which he had; and they cried out before him, "Bow the knee!" So he set him over all the land of Egypt. Pharaoh also said to Joseph, "I am Pharaoh, and without your consent no man may lift his hand or foot in all the land of

Egypt." NKJV.

13. O Lord, help me to return to You in truth, as my only source, in the name of Jesus.

Galatians 5:6
For in Christ Jesus neither circumcision nor uncircumcision avails anything, but faith working through love. NKJV

Galatians 5:13-16
For you, brethren, have been called to liberty; only do not use liberty as an opportunity for the flesh, but through love serve one another. 14 For all the law is fulfilled in one word, even in this: "You shall love your neighbor as yourself." 15 But if you bite and devour one another, beware lest you be consumed by one another! I say then: Walk in the Spirit, and you shall not fulfill the lust of the flesh. NKJV.

Galatians 5:22-25
But the fruit of the Spirit is love, joy, peace, long suffering, kindness, goodness, faithfulness, gentleness, self-control. Against such there is no law. And those who are Christ's have crucified the flesh with its passions and desires. If we live in the Spirit, let us also walk in the Spirit. NKJV

14. O Lord, let Your attributes increase in me-meekness, humility, love, holiness, integrity, uprightnes, consecration, purity, righteousness, faithfulness e.t.c

2 Corinthians 8:5
And not only as we had hoped, but they first gave themselves to the Lord, and then to us by the will of God. NKJV

Psalm51:16-19
For You do not desire sacrifice, or else I would give it; You do not

delight in burnt offering. The sacrifices of God are a broken spirit, A broken and a contrite heart ; These, O God, You will not despise. Do good in Your good pleasure to Zion; Build the walls of Jerusalem. Then You shall be pleased with the sacrifices of righteousness, With burnt offering and whole burnt offering; Then they shall offer bulls on Your altar. NKJV

15. O Lord, help me to willingly give myself to You without wavering in the name of Jesus.

Psalm 92:13-14
Those who are planted in the house of the Lord, Shall flourish in the courts of our God. They shall still bear fruit in old age; They shall be fresh and flourishing.

16. Lord, I know what moves You is the heart of a man. When my heart is tuned to You, my sacrifice becomes acceptable.
    * Help me to get connected to You and Your pleasures in the name of Jesus.
    * Help me to be there with You at all times, in the name of Jesus.

Psalm 1:1-3
Blessed is the man, Who walks not in the counsel of the ungodly, Nor stands in the path of sinners, Nor sits in the seat of the scornful; But his delight is in the law of the Lord, And in His law he meditates day and night. He shall be like a tree Planted by the rivers of water, That brings forth its fruit in its season, Whose leaf also shall not wither; And whatever he does shall prosper.

17. O Lord, help me to be deadly committed in the name of Jesus.

John 12:24-26
Most assuredly, I say to you, unless a grain of wheat falls into the ground and dies, it remains alone; but if it dies, it produces much grain. He who loves his life will lose it, and he who hates his life in this world will keep it for eternal life. If anyone serves Me, let him follow Me; and where I am, there My servant will be also. If anyone serves Me, him My Father will honor. NKJV

18. A man's yieldedness to God is what determines his results. O Lord, let my heart be planted in You and help secure my destiny as the only source, in the name of Jesus.

Ecclesiastes 9:4
But for him who is joined to all the living there is hope, for a living dog is better than a dead lion. NKJV

Romans 12:1
I beseech you therefore, brethren, by the mercies of God, that you present your bodies a living sacrifice, holy, acceptable to God, which is your reasonable service. NKJV

19. Father, help me grow up as a fruitful Christian that is thoroughly dedicated in the name of Jesus.

"Someone who can't pay tithe can't give his life. There is no truly dedicated person that does not find joy in giving material and monetary offerings. If he has given his life, his material possessions have no more value in his sight" -Dr. David Oyedepo

20. O Lord, help me that all my life will be lived pleasing You and promoting Your kingdom in the name of Jesus.
    * O Lord, lead me to a point of desperate surrenderedness, total yieldedness for Your true

colours to come forth in my life, in the name of Jesus.

21. If dedication makes one's life fertile and fruitful, If it makes a reasonable worshipper, and one's transformation to be sure...

* Lord help me to stay dedicated and stay planted in Your house.
* My eye will no more lose colour.
* I choose to stay consecrated and planted in the house of God.
* I will surely keep bringing forth fruits the remaining days of my life in the name of Jesus.

My kingdom commitment and connection will surely produce plenty. (evangelism, soul winning, serving in a unit with my talents, tithing, paying vows, fellowshipping etc. must be consistent).

Deuteronomy 28:47-48

"Because you did not serve the LORD your God with joy and gladness of heart, for the abundance of everything, "therefore you shall serve your enemies, whom the LORD will send against you, in hunger, in thirst, in nakedness, and in need of everything; and He will put a yoke of iron on your neck until He has destroyed you.

Jeremiah . 23:36-39

"And the oracle of the LORD you shall mention no more. For every man's word will be his oracle, for you have perverted the words of the living God, the LORD of hosts, our God. "Thus you shall say to the prophet, 'What has the LORD answered you?' and, 'What has the LORD spoken?' "But since you say, 'The oracle of the LORD!' therefore thus says the LORD: 'Because you say this word, "The oracle of the LORD!" and I have sent to you, saying, "Do not say, 'The oracle of the

LORD!'" 'therefore behold, I, even I, will utterly forget you and forsake you, and the city that I gave you and your fathers, and will cast you out of My presence".

22. O Lord, take me to the realm of delightsome commitments. i.e getting involved with excitement, in the name of Jesus.

1 Kings 3:3
And Solomon loved the LORD, walking in the statutes of his father David, except that he sacrificed and burned incense at the high places.

2 Corinthians 9:6-8
But this I say: He who sows sparingly will also reap sparingly, and he who sows bountifully will also reap bountifully. So let each one give as he purposes in his heart, not grudgingly or of necessity; for God loves a cheerful giver. And God is able to make all grace abound toward you, that you, always having all sufficiency in all things, may have an abundance for every good work.

Matthew 22:37
Jesus said to him, " 'You shall love the LORD your God with all your heart, with all your soul, and with all your mind.

23. O lord, make me to be mindful that You delight in cheerful givers.

John 21:15
So when they had eaten breakfast, Jesus said to Simon Peter, "Simon, son of Jonah, do you love Me more than these?" He said to Him, "Yes, Lord; You know that I love You." He said to him, "Feed My lambs."

1 Kings 3:1-5

Now Solomon made a treaty with Pharaoh king of Egypt, and married Pharaoh's daughter; then he brought her to the City of David until he had finished building his own house, and the house of the LORD, and the wall all around Jerusalem. Meanwhile the people sacrificed at the high places, because there was no house built for the name of the LORD until those days. And Solomon loved the LORD, walking in the statutes of his father David, except that he sacrificed and burned incense at the high places. Now the king went to Gibeon to sacrifice there, for that was the great high place: Solomon offered a thousand burnt offerings on that altar. At Gibeon the LORD appeared to Solomon in a dream by night; and God said, "Ask! What shall I give you?"

James 4:3

You ask and do not receive, because you ask amiss, that you may spend it on your pleasures.

24. O Lord, help me to love you crazily in the name of Jesus.

Proverbs 16:7

When a man's ways please the LORD, He makes even his enemies to be at peace with him.

25. O lord, help me to stay pleasing You in the name of Jesus.

1 Corinthians 13:3

And though I bestow all my goods to feed the poor, and though I give my body to be burned, but have not love, it profits me nothing.

26. Lord, help me to stay in love with You and in the affairs

of Your kingdom in the name of Jesus.

Proverbs 4:18
But the path of the just is like the shining sun, that shines ever brighter unto the perfect day.

27. Lord, let there be satisfactory progress in my destiny in the name of Jesus.
28. O Lord, whatever is out of place that is making my life unjust, reveal it and deliver me in the name of Jesus.

John 21:15
So when they had eaten breakfast, Jesus said to Simon Peter, "Simon, son of Jonah, do you love Me more than these?" He said to Him, "Yes, Lord; You know that I love You." He said to him, "Feed My lambs."

29. O Lord, deliver me from seeking You for my own sake in the name of Jesus.

Psalm 1:2
But his delight is in the law of the LORD, And in His law he meditates day and night.

Psalm 112:1-2
Praise the LORD! Blessed is the man who fears the LORD, Who delights greatly in His commandments. His descendants will be mighty on earth; The generation of the upright will be blessed.

30. Lord, give me a heart for You in the name of Jesus.

Psalm 34:10
The young lions lack and suffer hunger; But those who seek the LORD shall not lack any good thing

31. Lord, be my source for life in the name of Jesus.

Psalm 16:11
You will show me the path of life; In Your presence is fullness of joy; At Your right hand are pleasures forevermore.

1 Chronicles 29:2-3
"Now for the house of my God I have prepared with all my might: gold for things to be made of gold, silver for things of silver, bronze for things of bronze, iron for things of iron, wood for things of wood, onyx stones, stones to be set, glistening stones of various colors, all kinds of precious stones, and marble slabs in abundance. Moreover, because I have set my affection on the house of my God, I have given to the house of my God, over and above all that I have prepared for the holy house, my own special treasure of gold and silver:

Matthew 6:32-33
"For after all these things the Gentiles seek. For your heavenly Father knows that you need all these things. But seek first the kingdom of God and His righteousness, and all these things shall be added to you.

32. Grant me Your lasting prosperity with Your presence in the name of Jesus.

Psalm 37:4
Delight yourself also in the LORD, And He shall give you the desires of your heart.

John 14:21
"He who has My commandments and keeps them, it is he who loves Me. And he who loves Me will be loved by My Father, and I will love him and manifest Myself to him."

Romans 5:5
Now hope does not disappoint, because the love of God has been poured out in our hearts by the Holy Spirit who was given to us.

33. Teach me o Lord, to please you as my source for life.

MAKING A WAY WHERE THERE SEEMS TO BE NO WAY !

Yet I do proclaim a message of wisdom to those who are spiritually mature. But it is not the wisdom that belongs to this world or to the powers that rule this world; powers that are losing their power. The wisdom I proclaim is God's hidden wisdom, which he had already chosen for our glory even before the world was made. None of the rulers of this world knew this wisdom. If they had known it, they would not have crucified the Lord of glory. However, as the scripture says: "What no one ever saw or heard, what no one ever thought could happen, is the very thing God prepared for those who love him." But it was to us that God made known his secret by means of his Spirit. The Spirit searches everything, even the hidden depths of God's purposes. It is only the spirit within people that knows all about them; in the same way, only God's Spirit knows all about God. We have not received this world's spirit; instead, we have received the Spirit sent by God, so that we may know all that God has given us. So then, we do not speak in words taught by human wisdom, but in words taught by the Spirit, as we explain spiritual truths to those who have the Spirit. Whoever does not have the Spirit cannot receive the gifts that come from God's Spirit. Such people really do not understand them; they are nonsense to them, because their value can be judged only on a spiritual basis. Whoever has the Spirit, however, is able to judge the value of everything, but no one is able to judge him. As the scripture says: "Who knows the mind of the Lord? Who is able to give him advice?" We, however, have the mind of Christ. (1 Corinthians 2:6-16 GNB)

1. O Lord, make way for me where there seems to be no way, in the name of Jesus.
2. O Lord, endow me with Your supernatural wisdom to make a way for me where there seems to be no way, in the name of Jesus.
3. O Lord, grant unto me the capacity building for greater heights in Your new path of glory, in the name of Jesus.
4. O Lord, teach me in the path of righteousness all the days of my life and ministry, in the name of Jesus.

Joshua 14:6-15

One day some people from the tribe of Judah came to Joshua at Gilgal. One of them, Caleb son of Jephunneh the Kenizzite, said to him, "You know what the Lord said in Kadesh Barnea about you and me to Moses, the man of God. I was forty years old when the Lord 's servant Moses sent me from Kadesh Barnea to spy out this land. I brought an honest report back to him. The men who went with me, however, made our people afraid. But I faithfully obeyed the Lord my God. Because I did, Moses promised me that my children and I would certainly receive as our possession the land which I walked over. But now, look. It has been 45 years since the Lord said that to Moses. That was when Israel was going through the desert, and the Lord, as he promised, has kept me alive ever since. Look at me! I am 85 years old and I'm just as strong today as I was when Moses sent me out. I am still strong enough for war or for anything else. Now then, give me the hill country that the Lord promised me on that day when my men and I reported. We told you then that the race of giants called the Anakim were there in large walled cities. Maybe the Lord will be with me, and I will drive them out, just as the Lord said." Joshua blessed Caleb son of Jephunneh and gave him the city of Hebron as his possession. Hebron still belongs to the descendants of Caleb son of Jephunneh the Kenizzite, because he faithfully obeyed the Lord, the God of Israel. Before this, Hebron was called the city of Arba. (Arba had been the greatest of the Anakim.) There was now peace in the land. (Joshua 14:6-15 GNB)

5. O Lord, grant unto me as an individual, family, ministry, organization our own Hebron in the name of Jesus.

6. O Lord, as I am growing in life, ministry, business etc make me a person of influence with a positive difference in the name of Jesus.

7. O Lord, let my conviction in You and Your ability not be shaken irrespective of circumstance ,or situation around me in the name of Jesus.

8. O Lord, help me to manifest the FULNESS of Your strong character (integrity) without compromise all the days of my life, in the name of Jesus.

9. O Lord, help me to hold unto whatever You give or assign to me consistently (ministry, spiritual , strong character) for good in the name of Jesus.

10. O Lord, rebuild my confidence in You without me wavering in the name of Jesus.

11. O Lord, give me grace and faith to be unshakeable in You all the days of my life and ministry in the name of Jesus.

12. O Lord, help me to be consistent in my walk with You all the days of my life and ministry, in the name of Jesus.

13. O Lord, help me not to bend my Christian character to please any man in the name of Jesus.
14. O Lord, help me not to be a victim of this end time "pseudo churches" in the name of Jesus.
15. O Lord, make a way for me where there seems to be no way; spiritually, financially, ministerially, maritally, academically, physically, materially, health wise, career wise in the name of Jesus.

1 Corinthians . 16:9
There is a real opportunity here for great and worthwhile work, even though there are many opponents. (1 Corinthians 16:9) GNB

16. O Lord, grant unto me real opportunities for great and worthwhile works, irrespective of the many opponents, in the name of Jesus.

Matthew 14:22-32
Then Jesus made the disciples get into the boat and go on ahead to the other side of the lake, while he sent the people away. After sending the people away, he went up a hill by himself to pray. When evening came, Jesus was there alone; and by this time the boat was far out in the lake, tossed about by the waves, because the wind was blowing against it. Between three and six o'clock in the morning Jesus came to the disciples, walking on the water. When they saw him walking on the water, they were terrified. "It's a ghost!" they said, and screamed with fear. Jesus spoke to them at once. "Courage!" he said. "It is I. Don't be afraid!" Then Peter spoke up. "Lord, if it is really you, order me to come out on the water to you." "Come!" answered Jesus. So Peter got out of the boat and started walking on the water to Jesus. But when he noticed the strong wind, he was afraid and

started to sink down in the water. "Save me, Lord!" he cried. At once Jesus reached out and grabbed hold of him and said, "How little faith you have! Why did you doubt?" They both got into the boat, and the wind died down. Then the disciples in the boat worshipped Jesus. "Truly you are the Son of God!" they exclaimed. (Matthew 14:22-33 GNB)

17. O Lord, You are the God of unlimited possibilities, manifest Your unlimited possibilities in my life, family, business, ministry, assignments , career , academics etc in the name of Jesus.

18. O Lord, put an end to every storm in my way to good success as an individual, family, ministry, business, career etc in the name of Jesus .

19. O Lord ,order me out of the water to the other side where You are for life, in the name of Jesus.

20. O Lord, save me from every sinking and stinking situation of my life, ministry, career , and destiny in the name of Jesus.

21. Every storm and evil wind hindering the full worship of my God, die completely now in the name of Jesus.

22. Every wind of delay, wastage, limitation, and retardation in my voyage of life, ministry, career and destiny be wasted now in the name of Jesus.

23. Thou wind of the Spirit, carry me to the FULNESS of my God ordained purpose and destiny in the name of Jesus.

24. Father I thank You for making a way for me where there seems to be no way, in the name of Jesus.

REMEMBER ME O LORD!

"Remember me, Lord, when you help your people; include me

when you save them. Let me see the prosperity of your people and share in the happiness of your nation, in the glad pride of those who belong to you. (Psalms 106:4-5 GNB)

1. O Lord, remember me, my family, ministry, business etc with Your goodness in the name of Jesus.
2. O Lord, let me see and partake of the prosperity of Your people in the name of Jesus.
3. O Lord, let me share in the happiness of Your nations in the name of Jesus.
4. O Lord, let me partake in the glad pride (inheritance) of those who belong to You in the name of Jesus.

Jude 1:14-22

It was Enoch, the seventh direct descendant from Adam, who long ago prophesied this about them: "The Lord will come with many thousands of his holy angels to bring judgement on all, to condemn them all for the godless deeds they have performed and for all the terrible words that godless sinners have spoken against him!" These people are always grumbling and blaming others; they follow their own evil desires; they boast about themselves and flatter others in order to get their own way. But remember, my friends, what you were told in the past by the apostles of our Lord Jesus Christ. They said to you, "When the last days come, people will appear who will mock you, people who follow their own godless desires." These are the people who cause divisions, who are controlled by their natural desires, who do not have the Spirit. But you, my friends, keep on building yourselves up on your most sacred faith. Pray in the power of the Holy Spirit, and keep yourselves in the love of God, as you wait for our Lord Jesus Christ in his mercy to give you eternal life. Show mercy towards those who have doubts; save others by snatching them out of the fire; and to others show mercy mixed with fear, but hate their very clothes, stained by their sinful lusts. (Jude 1:14-23 GNB)

5. O Lord, have mercy on me and deliver me from the judgement of the godless words I have spoken, deeds I have done against You, Your interests etc in the name of Jesus.

6. O Lord, forgive me for always grumbling and blaming others for my own evil desires I have followed, in the name of Jesus.

7. O Lord, deliver me from every self boasting, and flattering of others in order to get my way in the name of Jesus.

8. O Lord, help me to build my self in the Holy Ghost and in Your love in the name of Jesus.

9. O Lord I, ask for the inflow of Your eternal life without ceasing in the name of Jesus.

10. O Lord, use me to show mercy to those who have doubts and to snatch them out of fire in the name of Jesus.

11. O Lord, deliver us from our filthy garments, sinful lust and diverse fears in the name of Jesus.

12. O Lord remember me with Your new proofs, grace, power, blessings in this new season in the name of Jesus.

"As they approached Jerusalem, near the towns of Bethphage and Bethany, they came to the Mount of Olives. Jesus sent two of his disciples on ahead with these instructions: "Go to the village there ahead of you. As soon as you get there, you will find a colt tied up that has never been ridden. Untie it and bring it here. And if someone asks you why you are doing that, tell him that the Master needs it and will send it back at once." So

they went and found a colt out in the street, tied to the door of a house. As they were untying it, some of the bystanders asked them, "What are you doing, untying that colt?" They answered just as Jesus had told them, and the bystanders let them go. They brought the colt to Jesus, threw their cloaks over the animal, and Jesus got on. Many people spread their cloaks on the road, while others cut branches in the fields and spread them on the road. The people who were in front and those who followed behind began to shout, "Praise God! God bless him who comes in the name of the Lord! God bless the coming kingdom of King David, our father! Praise God!" Jesus entered Jerusalem, went into the Temple, and looked round at everything. But since it was already late in the day, he went out to Bethany with the twelve disciples. (Mark 11:1-11 GNB)

13. O Lord, help me to untie whatever needs to be untied (for my success) in life, family, ministry, business, destiny in the name of Jesus.

14. O Lord, use me for Your glory locally, nationally, intercontinentally, internationally and globally in the name of Jesus.

15. O Lord, help me not to hold back my seeds and instruments of blessings in the name of Jesus.

16. O Lord, find rest in me, my family, ministry, resources, and destiny in the name of Jesus.

Matthew 16:18
And so I tell you, Peter: you are a rock, and on this rock foundation I will build my church, and not even death will ever be able to overcome it. (Matthew 16:18 GNB)

17. O Lord, build Your church, temple, kingdom and let not the gate of hell prevail in the name of Jesus.

Matthew 28:18-20

Jesus drew near and said to them, "I have been given all authority in heaven and on earth. Go, then, to all peoples everywhere and make them my disciples: baptize them in the name of the Father, the Son, and the Holy Spirit, and teach them to obey everything I have commanded you. And I will be with you always, to the end of the age." (Matthew 28:18-20 GNB)

18. O Lord, draw me nearer to thee and declare the intents of Your heart without ceasing in the name of Jesus.

19. Thank You Lord, for remembering me, my family, my ministry, my academics, job etc with Your end time power, in the name of Jesus.

20. O Lord, I demand for more power, authority and proofs in heaven and earth without ceasing, to make a disciple of all nations without stress and distractions in the name of Jesus.

    * I declare the eyes of God upon you, His ears tuned in to your cry in Jesus name.

    * I declare that you live in the secret place of the most high and abide under His feathers, and under His wings you are protected in Jesus name !

SUPERNATURAL EXPLOITS

1. Everything that is void in my life, let Your light shine over them.

2. O Lord, let there be divine announcement of my positive changes in Jesus name.

3. Overturn everything that needs to be turned in my life, finance, marriage, business, ministry etc.

4. Flood gate of my joy open unto me, my family etc.

5. The era of lack is over in my life, business etc. I enter into my season of fulfillment in Jesus name.

6. O Lord, raise help for me in Jesus name.

7. Whatever that is covering my glory, I command you to scatter in the name of Jesus.

8. Establish Your covenant of glorification in me in Jesus name.

9. Grace and glory will not lack in my life, marriage, business, work etc.

10. Let Your glory overshadow my life, Church etc.

11. Give unto me authoritative standing in life, ministry etc.

12. The tree of my glory will not dry in Jesus name.

13. The Lord will rebuild every crack in the wall of my glory.

14. O Lord, grant me open heavens. Cause doors to open unto me in high places in the name of Jesus.

15. O Lord, let there be manifestation of Your promises in my life, family, ministry etc in the name of Jesus.

16. Let Your spirit move over my life, marriage, children and career in Jesus name.

17. Lord use me for Your glory.

18. God of Elijah let Your fire fall on me.

19. My Lord and my God, let Your Spirit be obvious in my life.

20. Let Your Spirit come upon me afresh in Jesus name.

21. Whatever will not make Your use of me to be effective, take it away in the name of Jesus.

22. If You can use anything Lord, use me beyond measure in Jesus name.

23. Do what eyes have not seen in my life, o Lord.

24. Let all my enemies be scattered in Jesus name.

25. I call forth supernatural exploits into my life, family, ministry etc in the name of Jesus.

26. O Lord, make an open show of all my adversaries in Jesus name.

27. O Lord, enlarge my coast exceeding greatly, in the name of Jesus.

28. Fill me, my family etc. with Your Spirit in the name of Jesus.

29. O Lord, Empower me to bring good news to the people in the name of Jesus.

30. O Lord, Empower me to heal the broken hearted in the name of Jesus.

31. O Lord, use me to announce Your blessing, glory etc in the name of Jesus.

32. O Lord put an end to every shame in my life and destiny, in the name of Jesus.

33. O Lord, touch me for global impact in Jesus name

34. O Lord, redeem me from small manifestations to greater ones in Jesus name.

35. Every contending power against me, family, breakthrough, health etc. break in Jesus name.

36. (Demand for new things.) Lord let there be a new opening concerning my ministry, business etc.

37. Father, the miracles you have promised to bring to pass in my life, bring them to pass in Jesus name.

38. Open the heavens and open doors over my needs in ministry, family, business, career in Jesus name.

39. Whatever high position you have reserved for me, no man will take my place in Jesus name.

40. Lord repair the... in my life, family etc. (mention your lapses)

41. Everything that You need to finish, Lord finish them in

Jesus name.

42. Mend my broken walls and fences.

43. O Lord, Wash me with Your liquid in the name of Jesus.

44. O Lord, let Your joy overflow in my life, ministry, business etc.

45. O God of salvation, give to me now my benefits.

46. O Lord, let there be divine provision

47. Power for fruit of the womb that turns barrenness to fruitfulness give it to me o Lord.

48. The power you gave to Elijah and Elisha, give it to me o Lord.

49. The power that re-creates, Lord give it to me.

50. The power that makes a way where there is no way, that parted the red sea, give it to me.

51. Father give unto me power for change.

52. O Lord, give unto my glory a voice.

53. My glory, breakthrough and break forth in Jesus name

54. Lord I ask for Your supernatural help.

55. My glory will not fade away like smoke in Jesus name.

56. Lord I put confusion in the midst of every power that is monitoring and contending with my glory.

57. Every tree in my life that is dry, come alive in Jesus name.

58. O Lord, give unto me the power that cures the incurable.

59. According to *Deuteronomy. 8:18;* Supernatural power to get wealth, give it to me

60. Begin to thank God for answered prayers.

UNLIMITED BREAKTHROUGHS

But now to continue; the son who will receive his father's property is treated just like a slave while he is young, even though he really owns everything. While he is young, there are men who take care of him and manage his affairs until the time set by his father. In the same way, we too were slaves of the ruling spirits of the universe before we reached spiritual maturity. But when the right time finally came, God sent his own Son. He came as the son of a human mother and lived under the Jewish Law, to redeem those who were under the Law, so that we might become God's sons and daughters. To show that you are his sons and daughters, God sent the Spirit of his Son into our hearts, the Spirit who cries out, "Father, my Father." So then, you are no longer a slave but a son or daughter. And since that is what you are, God will give you all that he has for his heirs. (Galatians 4:1-7 GNB)

1.   O Lord help me to grow unto spiritual understanding and maturity so as to possess all You have provided for me and my interests as Your joint heir, in the name of Jesus.

The world and all that is in it belong to the Lord; the earth and all who live on it are his. He built it on the deep waters beneath the earth and laid its foundations in the ocean depths. Who has the right to go up the Lord 's hill? Who may enter his holy Temple? Those who are pure in act and in thought, who do not worship idols or make false promises. The Lord will bless them and save them; God will declare them innocent. Such are the people who come to God, who come into the presence of the God of Jacob. Fling wide the gates, open the ancient doors, and the great king will come in. Who is this great king? He is the Lord, strong and mighty, the Lord, victorious in battle. Fling wide the gates, open the ancient doors, and the great king will come in. Who is this great king? The triumphant Lord; he is the great king! (Psalms 24:1-10 GNB)

2. O Lord, qualify me to posses my possessions in full measure in the name of Jesus.

3. O Lord, purify my actions and thoughts for new heights in life, business and ministry (locally, nationally, intercontinentally, globally) In the mighty name of Jesus.

4. Lift up your heads, o ye gates ! fling open you ancient doors! Let the triumphant King come into my affairs, ministry, family, career, business etc in the name of Jesus.

5. O Lord, crown all my pursuits on this earth with favour, blessing, goodness, mercy, joy, peace, prosperity breakthroughs etc in the name of Jesus.

Jesus drank the wine and said, "It is finished!" Then he bowed his head and died. (John 19:30 GNB)

6. Father, You gave Your only begotten son as a ransom to finish my battles, challenges, pains and limitations over 2000 years ago. Let ALL see the finished product of The Ransom (The Lord Jesus) in my life, my family, my ministry, my business etc in the name of Jesus.

But thanks be to God! For in union with Christ we are always led by God as prisoners in Christ's victory procession. God uses us to make the knowledge about Christ spread everywhere like a sweet fragrance. For we are like a sweet-smelling incense offered by Christ to God, which spreads among those who are being saved and those who are being lost. For those who are being lost, it is a deadly stench that kills; but for those who are being saved, it is a fragrance that brings life. Who, then, is capable of such a task? We are not like so many others, who handle God's message as if it were cheap merchandise; but because God has sent us, we speak with sincerity in his presence, as servants of Christ. (2 Corinthians 2:14-17 GNB)

7. Father, I acknowledge Your mercy over me. Thank You for answering me always.

8. Thank You Jesus for the triumphant victories at all time in my life, business, ministry, family and all endeavors.

9. O Lord, I thank You for using me as Your sweet smelling fragrance that brings life to both the saved and the lost.

10. O Lord, sanctify me, my family, my destiny, my business, my finance, my home, my marriage, my projects etc in the name of Jesus.

Joshua then told the two men who had served as spies, "Go into the prostitute's house and bring her and her family out, as you promised her." So they went and brought Rahab out, along with her father and mother, her brothers, and the rest of her family. They took them all, family and slaves, to safety near the Israelite camp. Then they set fire to the city and burnt it to the ground, along with everything in it, except the things made of gold, silver, bronze, and iron, which they took and put in the Lord's treasury. But Joshua spared the lives of the prostitute Rahab and all her relatives, because she had hidden the two spies that he had sent to Jericho. (Her descendants have lived in Israel to this day.) At that time Joshua issued a solemn warning: "Anyone who tries to rebuild the city of Jericho will be under the Lord's curse. Whoever lays the foundation will lose his eldest son; Whoever builds the gates will lose his youngest." So the Lord was with Joshua, and his fame spread through the whole country. (Joshua 6:22-27 GNB)

11. O Lord, help me to fulfill purpose without being self centered, unwilling, disobedient, covenant breaking, procrastinating etc in the name of Jesus.

12. O Lord, You had mercy on Rahab and all her family members, have mercy on me and all members of my family, ministry, business, helpers of my destiny and messengers of Joy in the name of Jesus.

13. Father, whatever I am building, or rebuilding that is not of Jesus Christ, Lord deliver me from the path of destruction, in the name of Jesus.

14. O Lord, as You were with Joshua and he was fulfilled, be with me for good success, fulfillment and greater exploits in the name of Jesus.

15. O Lord, grant unto me an everlasting productive insight all the days of my life, ministry, destiny etc in the name of Jesus.

16. O Lord, manifest Yourself through me as a "barrier breaker" in all my endeavors in the name of Jesus.

I look to the mountains; where will my help come from? My help will come from the Lord, who made heaven and earth. He will not let you fall; your protector is always awake. The protector of Israel never dozes or sleeps. The Lord will guard you; he is by your side to protect you. The sun will not hurt you during the day, nor the moon during the night. The Lord will protect you from all danger; he will keep you safe. He will protect you as you come and go now and for ever. (Psalms 121:1-8 GNB)

17. O Lord, send me help speedily from Your presence than ever before, in the name of Jesus.

18. O Lord, help me not fall spiritually, -ministerially, physically, financially, maritally, materially, bodily and in all wise in the name of Jesus.

19. O Lord, guard and protect me, my household ,family and they that favour my righteous cause in the name of Jesus.
20. O Lord, protect me and all that you have blessed me with in Jesus name.
21. O Lord give unto me the peculiar and unique anointing of "the barrier breaker" with ease in the name of Jesus.

God has raised from death our Lord Jesus, who is the Great Shepherd of the sheep as the result of his blood, by which the eternal covenant is sealed. May the God of peace provide you with every good thing you need in order to do his will, and may he, through Jesus Christ, do in us what pleases him. And to Christ be the glory for ever and ever! Amen. (Hebrews 13:20-21 GNB)

22. O Lord, The Great Shepherd, the one whose blood sealed off the Eternal covenant, give me everything to do Your will always in Jesus name.

Thank You Lord for answering my prayers. To you Lord , Jesus Christ be all the glory forever and ever Amen!

DIVINE INTERVENTION

That night Jacob got up and took his two wives, his two female servants and his eleven sons and crossed the ford of the Jabbok. After he had sent them across the stream, he sent over all his possessions. So Jacob was left alone, and a man wrestled with him till daybreak. When the man saw that he could not overpower him, he touched the socket of Jacob's hip so that his hip was wrenched as he wrestled with the man. Then the man said, "Let me go, for it is daybreak." But Jacob replied, "I will not let you go unless you bless me." The man asked him, "What is your name?" "Jacob," he answered. Then the man said, "Your name will no longer be Jacob, but Israel, because you have struggled with God and with humans and have overcome." Jacob said, "Please tell me your name." But he replied, "Why do you ask my name?" Then he blessed him there. So Jacob called the place Peniel, saying, "It is because I saw God face to face, and yet my life was spared." The sun rose above him as he passed Peniel, and he was limping because of his hip. Therefore to this day the Israelites do not eat the tendon attached to the socket of the hip, because the socket of Jacob's hip was touched near the tendon. (Genesis 32:22-32 NIV)

1. Bless me O Lord indeed exceeding mightily in the name of Jesus.

And Jabez was more honourable than his brethren: and his mother called his name Jabez, saying, Because I bare him with sorrow. And Jabez called on the God of Israel, saying, Oh that thou wouldest bless me indeed, and enlarge my coast, and that thine hand might be with me, and that thou wouldest keep me from evil, that it may not grieve me! And God granted him that which he requested. (1 Chronicles 4:9-10 KJV)

2a. O Lord, transform me for new results that man cannot have a gainsay about in the name of Jesus.

2b. Make me more honorable than them all in the name of Jesus.

3. O Lord, Jacob saw You"face to face", Jabez was transformed by Your mercy, Esther and Mordecai encountered the fruit Your divine providence, remember me for good. Let me see You face to face, so I can obtain mercy, to manifest divine providence and unprecedented favors in the name of Jesus.

4. O Lord, spare my life, my family, my ministry, my destiny and my businesses in the name of Jesus.

But thanks be to God! For in union with Christ we are always led by God as prisoners in Christ's victory procession. God uses us to make the knowledge about Christ spread everywhere like a sweet fragrance. For we are like a sweet-smelling incense offered by Christ to God, which spreads among those who are being saved and those who are being lost. (2 Corinthians 2:14-15 GNB)

5. Father, thank You for intervening to open uncommon doors of blessings, divine shift, divine utterances, testimonies and success for me, my spouse, my family, my helpers in the name of Jesus.

6. Father, thank You for leading me from place to place in one perpetual victory parade in the name of Jesus.

7. Father, use me to take the knowledge of Jesus Christ everywhere I go. Let the people breathe the exquisite fragrance that proceeds from Your presence in the name of Jesus.

8. Father, help me to stand in Christ's presence when I speak, as You look into my face, in the name of Jesus.

9. Father, grant me divine utterances straight from Your presence and help me to declare it honestly ,in season and out of season, in the name of Jesus.

The Pharisees heard that Jesus was making and baptizing more followers than John, although Jesus himself did not baptize people, but his followers did. Jesus knew that the Pharisees had heard about him, so he left Judea and went back to Galilee. But on the way he had to go through the country of Samaria. (John 4:1-4 NCV)

10. Lord Jesus, as you needed to pass through Samaria, pass through my life, my family, our churches, our ministries and our businesses in Jesus name.

11. O Lord, use me to open the gateway of nations for the explosion of Your good news in these last days, in the name of Jesus.

Proverbs 24:1-5, 9-10

Be not thou envious against evil men, neither desire to be with them. For their heart studieth destruction, and their lips talk of mischief. Through wisdom is an house builded; and by understanding it is established: And by knowledge shall the chambers be filled with all precious and pleasant riches. A wise man is strong; yea, a man of knowledge increaseth strength.

The thought of foolishness is sin: and the scorner is an abomination to men. If thou faint in the day of adversity, thy strength is small.

12. O Lord, grant me the ability to practically apply the little knowledge I have of walking with You and to increase the capacity for knowledge in the name of Jesus.

13. O Lord, in this new season, take time wasters and evil men away from my life, family, ministry, businesses, in the name of Jesus.

14. O Lord, fight my battles on all side and cause me to triumph victoriously in all my endeavors in the name of Jesus.

15. O Lord, as You divinely intervene in my affairs, enhance Your wisdom, understanding and revelation knowledge in me for the fulfillment of my destiny in Jesus name.

16. O Lord show me Your glory in the name of Jesus.
17. O Lord teach me Your ways in the name of Jesus.
18. O Lord, establish Your presence with me in the name of Jesus.

The Lord will perfect that which concerneth me: thy mercy, O Lord, endureth for ever: forsake not the works of thine own hands. (Psalm138:8 KJV)

19. O Lord, magnify Your name in all my endeavors in the name of Jesus
20. O Lord, I am the work of Your hand, do not forsake me in the name of Jesus.

Speak, ye that ride on white asses, ye that sit in judgment, and walk by the way. They that are delivered from the noise of archers in the places of drawing water, there shall they rehearse the righteous acts of the Lord, even the righteous acts toward the inhabitants of his villages in Israel: then shall the people of the Lord go down to the gates. Awake, awake, Deborah: awake, awake, utter a song: arise, Barak, and lead thy captivity captive, thou son of Abinoam. Then he made him that remaineth have dominion over the nobles among the people: the Lord made me have dominion over the mighty. (Judges 5:10-13 KJV).

21. O Lord, You made me have dominion over the mighty ; I therefore decree that an end has come to any force manifesting itself against my fulfillment in the name of Jesus.
22. O Lord, help me to be concerned above everything else with Your kingdom and what You require of me, like never before in the name of Jesus.
    O Lord touch me, touch my wife/husband, touch my

children , my businesses, my ministry, my destiny for good in the name of Jesus.

23. O Lord, help me to seek You and Your righteousness; as I do, open the flood gate of heaven and open a new a book of remembrance for me, my wife, my children, my ministry and helpers of my destiny in the name of Jesus.

24. O Lord, honour Your words and Your ways in my life, my ministry and my destiny in the name of Jesus.

25. O Lord, establish Your fresh fire and new baptism of the fire of Your Spirit in me in the mighty name of Jesus.

26. Begin to thank Him for divinely intervening in your affairs, family, businesses, spouse, children, ministry, assignments and mandate!

OPEN HEAVENS

1. O Lord , let the heavens over me be opened in the name of Jesus.

2. I come against every ritualistic sacrifice of children in our nation in the name of Jesus.

You also will command nations you do not know, and peoples unknown to you will come running to obey, because I, the LORD your God, the Holy One of Israel, have made you glorious." (Isaiah 55:5 NLT)

3. I command nations and people known and unknown to come running to obey me , in the name of Jesus.

4. O Lord, if I have found grace in Your sight , show that You have made me glorious, in the name of Jesus .

5. Father Glorify Your name in my favour in all the earth in Jesus name.

No curse can touch Jacob; no magic has any power against Israel. For now it will be said of Jacob, 'What wonders God has done for Israel!' (Numbers 23:23 NLT)

6. O Lord, let the wickedness of the wicked against me, my family, ministry, helpers, and my messengers of joy return back to senders in the name of Jesus.

Rise up, O God, and scatter your enemies. Let those who hate God run for their lives. Blow them away like smoke. Melt them like wax in a fire. Let the wicked perish in the presence of God. But let the godly rejoice. Let them be glad in God's presence. Let them be filled with joy.

7. Rise up O Lord and scatter Your enemies(in my life, family, ministry, business, marriage, churches, outreaches) in the name of Jesus.
8. O Lord, let all Your enemies perish and melt like wax in fire, in the name of Jesus.
9. O Lord, fill me with Your joy unspeakable, full of the Holy Ghost in the name of Jesus.
10. Any wicked habitation in my neighborhood, catch fire in the name of Jesus.
11. Every power hindering the speed of my liftings and accomplishments in life and ministry, be destroyed in Jesus name.
12. O Lord, grant me unprecedented divine speed for my accelerated liftings and accomplishments in life and ministry in the name of of Jesus.

"Bring all the tithes into the storehouse so there will be enough food in my Temple. If you do," says the LORD of Heaven's Armies, "I will open the windows of heaven for you. I will pour

out a blessing so great you won't have enough room to take it in!
Try it! Put me to the test! Your crops will be abundant, for I will
guard them from insects and disease. Your grapes will not fall
from the vine before they are ripe," says the LORD of Heaven's
Armies. "Then all nations will call you blessed, for your land
will be such a delight," says the LORD of Heaven's Armies.
(Malachi 3:10-12 NLT)

13. The heavens over my family, finances, health, ministry, outreaches, journey be opened in the name of Jesus.
14. O Lord, open the door of my joy in the name of Jesus.
15. O Lord, keep away evil deeds and reports from me, my family, my ministry, outreaches etc in the name of Jesus.
16. O Lord, what gives me joy let it not bring me sorrow, sadness and pain in the name of Jesus.
17. Father in the name of Jesus, take me into the throne of Your power, honour, favour, greatness, breakthrough, success, abundance, and riches of Grace in the name of Jesus.
18. Father, give unto me Your Almighty power, in the name of Jesus.
19. Father, grant me the fire power and the grace to hear the inaudible, to see the unseeable and to make the impossible possible in the name of Jesus.
20. Speak to me Lord Jesus, I want to hear from You!
21. Father, let me enjoy the fire that proceeds from Your presence for signs, wonders, miracles, blessings, strange acts in the name of Jesus.
22. Father, give unto me power and fire for unlimited possibilities supernaturally in the name of Jesus.
23. O Lord, use me for Your glory without ceasing in the name of Jesus.

"I tell you the truth, anyone who believes in me will do the same works I have done, and even greater works, because I am going to be with the Father. You can ask for anything in my name, and I will do it, so that the Son can bring glory to the Father. Yes, ask me for anything in my name, and I will do it! (John 14:12-14 NLT)

24. Lord Jesus, grant unto me multiple portions of Your grace and power for greater works in the name of Jesus.
25. Every stronghold in my family that will not let the power of God flow freely in my life and ministry, I decree death unto you in the name of Jesus.
26. Father, I thank You for making the crooked way straight. In the name of Jesus.
27. Thank You Jesus for the Open heavens over me in Jesus name.

THE RESURRECTION POWER

As they were going out, they met a man from Cyrene named Simon, and the soldiers forced him to carry Jesus' cross. They came to a place called Golgotha, which means, "The Place of the Skull". There they offered Jesus wine mixed with a bitter substance; but after tasting it, he would not drink it. They crucified him and then divided his clothes among them by throwing dice. After that they sat there and watched him. Above his head they put the written notice of the accusation against him: "This is Jesus, the King of the Jews." Then they crucified two bandits with Jesus, one on his right and the other on his left. People passing by shook their heads and hurled insults at Jesus: "You were going to tear down the Temple and build it up again in three days! Save yourself if you are God's Son! Come on down from the cross!" In the same way the chief priests and the teachers of the Law and the elders jeered at him: "He saved others, but he cannot save himself! Isn't he the king of Israel? If he comes down off the cross now, we will believe in him! He trusts in God and claims to be God's Son. Well, then, let us see if God wants to save him now!" Even the bandits who had been crucified with him insulted him in the same way. (Matthew 27:32-44 GNB)

1. O Lord, for all the shame, pains, poisons, insults, mockery, and crucifixion You suffered for me, let it manifest multiples of redemption benefits in my life, family, ministry, business, career etc in the name of Jesus. *(Revelation 5:12)*
2. O Lord, manifest the FULNESS of the benefits of Your suffering, death, resurrection for our total victory, and liftings (spiritually, financially, materially, academically. Ministerially, career wise etc) in the name of Jesus.

At noon the whole country was covered with darkness, which lasted for three hours. At about three o'clock Jesus cried out with a loud shout, Eli, Eli, lema sabachthani?" which means, "My God, my God, why did you abandon me?" Some of the people standing there heard him and said, "He is calling for Elijah!" One of them ran up at once, took a sponge, soaked it in cheap wine, put it on the end of a stick, and tried to make him drink it. But the others said, "Wait, let us see if Elijah is coming to save him!" Jesus again gave a loud cry and breathed his last. Then the curtain hanging in the Temple was torn in two from top to bottom. The earth shook, the rocks split apart, the graves broke open, and many of God's people who had died were raised to life. They left the graves, and after Jesus rose from death, they went into the Holy City, where many people saw them. When the army officer and the soldiers with him who were watching Jesus saw the earthquake and everything else that happened, they were terrified and said, "He really was the Son of God!" There were many women there, looking on from a distance, who had followed Jesus from Galilee and helped him. Among them were Mary Magdalene, Mary the mother of James and Joseph, and the wife of Zebedee. (Matthew 27:45-56 GNB)

3. O Lord, by the reason of the dark hours you have suffered, every dark hour in my life, -family, -ministry, -business, -health, career etc be no more in the name of Jesus.

4. By reason of the temple veil that parted into two from top to bottom, when You gave up the ghost at Calvary; O Lord, let all veils, obstacles, barriers, limitations and hindrances before me, my family, my destiny give way now in the name of Jesus.

5. Father, by the power that made the earth to shake, rocks to split, graves to break open and Jesus to arise from the dead, let this power work wonders, blessings, miracles, signs, breakthroughs, exceeding and triumphant total victory in my life, my family, my business, my academics, my carrier, my ministry and my destiny in the name of Jesus.

6. Father, with terrific infallible proofs before the people, they all acknowledged that truly Jesus is the Son of God. Endorse my destiny with infallible proofs, for Your glory in the name of Jesus.

7. Father, You raised human helpers for Jesus. By His resurrection power, raise numerous helpers for me, my family, my ministry, my career etc in the name of Jesus.

When it was evening, a rich man from Arimathea arrived; his name was Joseph, and he also was a disciple of Jesus. He went into the presence of Pilate and asked for the body of Jesus. Pilate gave orders for the body to be given to Joseph. So Joseph took it, wrapped it in a new linen sheet, and placed it in his own tomb, which he had just recently dug out of solid rock. Then he rolled a large stone across the entrance to the tomb and went away. Mary Magdalene and the other Mary were sitting there, facing the tomb. (Matthew 27:57-61 GNB)

8. O Lord, by Your resurrection power, make my life, ministry, family, career, destiny etc more glorious and honorable to the end in the name of Jesus.
9. Despite all the moves of the enemy to subvert Your will in the destiny of Jesus Christ, it all failed.
   Father, by the resurrection power of Jesus Christ, uphold Your promises, blessings, and counsels in righteousness for me, my family, my ministry, my career in the name of Jesus.

After the Sabbath, as Sunday morning was dawning, Mary Magdalene and the other Mary went to look at the tomb. Suddenly there was a violent earthquake; an angel of the Lord came down from heaven, rolled the stone away, and sat on it. His appearance was like lightning, and his clothes were white as snow. The guards were so afraid that they trembled and became like dead men. The angel spoke to the women. "You must not be afraid," he said. "I know you are looking for Jesus, who was crucified. He is not here; he has been raised, just as he said. Come here and see the place where he was lying. Go quickly now, and tell his disciples, 'He has been raised from death, and now he is going to Galilee ahead of you; there you will see him!' Remember what I have told you." So they left the tomb in a hurry, afraid and yet filled with joy, and ran to tell his disciples. Suddenly Jesus met them and said, "Peace be with you." They came up to him, took hold of his feet, and worshipped him. "Do not be afraid," Jesus said to them. "Go and tell my brothers to go to Galilee, and there they will see me." (Matthew 28:1-10 GNB)

10. O Lord, by virtue of Your resurrection, take away my reproaches, my limitations, my pains, my infirmities, my insensitivity of the Spirit, my foolishness etc in the name of Jesus.

11. O Lord, whatever is in me, my family, business, ministry, career that ought not to die that is dying or dead, by Your resurrection power, let them come alive fully now in the name of Jesus.

12. O Lord, the peace You gave by Your resurrection that expresses progress, prosperity, fulfillment in all things, manifest greater peace in me, family, ministry, career and destiny in the name of Jesus.

13. Lord Jesus, when the disciples met You after Your resurrection, You granted them boldness and access to spread the good news. O Lord grant me boldness, and access to be used for the spread of the good news, in the name of Jesus.

14. Resurrection power of the Lord, do terrific things in righteousness for me, with me, and through me without ceasing in the name of Jesus.

While the women went on their way, some of the soldiers guarding the tomb went back to the city and told the chief priests everything that had happened. The chief priests met with the elders and made their plan; they gave a large sum of money to the soldiers and said, "You are to say that his disciples came during the night and stole his body while you were asleep. And if the Governor should hear of this, we will convince him that you are innocent, and you will have nothing to worry about." The guards took the money and did what they were told to do. And so that is the report spread round by the Jews to this very day. (Matthew 28:11-15 GNB)

15. Father, as You made the lies of the guards and the enemies of Jesus Christ to be null and void, O Lord put an end to every lie of the devil rearing its ugly head in all my interests and endeavors in the name of Jesus.

16. O Lord, let the FULNESS of Your power and authority in heaven and on earth show forth in my life and assignments forever in the name of Jesus.

17. O Lord, do new works of mercy and wonders in my life, family, ministry and destiny in the name of Jesus.

18. O Lord, everything about You is Love, by Your mercy, let Your overwhelming Love be on the increase in my life, family, ministry, relationships etc in the name of Jesus.

19. O Lord, I thank You for the everlasting life giving Spirit and power at work in us .

SEEKING THE KINGDOM ADVANCEMENT

"Seek the Kingdom of God above all else, and live righteously, and he will give you everything you need. (Matthew 6:33 NLT

"Don't store up treasures here on earth, where moths eat them and rust destroys them, and where thieves break in and steal. Store your treasures in heaven, where moths and rust cannot destroy, and thieves do not break in and steal. Wherever your treasure is, there the desires of your heart will also be. "Your eye is a lamp that provides light for your body. When your eye is

good, your whole body is filled with light. But when your eye is bad, your whole body is filled with darkness. And if the light you think you have is actually darkness, how deep that darkness is! "No one can serve two masters. For you will hate one and love the other; you will be devoted to one and despise the other. You cannot serve both God and money. "That is why I tell you not to worry about everyday life; whether you have enough food and drink, or enough clothes to wear. Isn't life more than food, and your body more than clothing? Look at the birds. They don't plant or harvest or store food in barns, for your heavenly Father feeds them. And aren't you far more valuable to him than they are? Can all your worries add a single moment to your life? "And why worry about your clothing? Look at the lilies of the field and how they grow. They don't work or make their clothing, yet Solomon in all his glory was not dressed as beautifully as they are. And if God cares so wonderfully for wild flowers that are here today and thrown into the fire tomorrow, he will certainly care for you. Why do you have so little faith? "So don't worry about these things, saying, 'What will we eat? What will we drink? What will we wear?' These things dominate the thoughts of unbelievers, but your heavenly Father already knows all your needs. (Matthew 6:19-32 NLT)

1. O Lord, help me to seek Your kingdom and righteousness without ceasing, in the name of Jesus.
2. Holy Spirit, grant me speed to accomplish new territories for the Kingdom of our Lord globally.
3. O Lord, if You can use anything, use me for Your glory like never before.
4. O Lord, Help me to seek Your face than ever before now.

5. O Lord, let Your plan for my destiny in line with Your kingdom agenda for me *(Jeremiah 29:11-13),* come to pass speedily in the name of Jesus.

Seek the Lord while he may be found; call on him while he is near. Let the wicked forsake their ways and the unrighteous their thoughts. Let them turn to the Lord, and he will have mercy on them, and to our God, for he will freely pardon. "For my thoughts are not your thoughts, neither are your ways my ways," declares the Lord. "As the heavens are higher than the earth, so are my ways higher than your ways and my thoughts than your thoughts. As the rain and the snow come down from heaven, and do not return to it without watering the earth and making it bud and flourish, so that it yields seed for the sower and bread for the eater, so is my word that goes out from my mouth: It will not return to me empty, but will accomplish what I desire and achieve the purpose for which I sent it. You will go out in joy and be led forth in peace; the mountains and hills will burst into song before you, and all the trees of the field will clap their hands. Instead of the thorn bush will grow the juniper, and instead of briers the myrtle will grow. This will be for the Lord's renown, for an everlasting sign, that will endure forever." (Isaiah 55:6-13 NIV)

6. O Lord, help me to find You in season and out of season in the name of Jesus.

7. O Lord, purify my mind and my thoughts in the name of Jesus.

8. O Lord, re-fire my passion for Your kingdom advancement in the name of Jesus.

9. O Lord, turn my sorrow to joy. Pains to profit lack to abundance, stagnation to advancement for Your name's sake in the name of Jesus.

10. O Lord, establish me in the light of Your truth as Your light bearer for the kingdom advancement in the name of Jesus.

11. O Lord, help me that my love for You will not grow cold, in the name of Jesus.

12. O Lord, take away anything hindering my trust, confidence and unshakeable believe in you in the name of Jesus.

13. O Lord, enhance my faith for Your Kingdom advancement with signs, wonders, and miracles following in the name of Jesus.

14. O Lord, approve of Your life in me (ministerially, spiritually, supernaturally, financially, maritally, economically, numerically etc) for Your kingdom advancement, in the name of Jesus.

15. O Lord, inoculate my faith afresh for Your Kingdom advancement in the name of Jesus.

16. O Lord revive me for Your kingdom advancement in the name of Jesus.

17. O Lord, grant unto us the right officers for the next move of Your Kingdom advancement in the name of Jesus.

18. Father open my eyes to see the unseeable, my ear to hear the inaudible. Give me power to make the impossible possible in righteousness for Your kingdom advancement, in the name of Jesus.

19. O Lord, grant me all round divine fulfillment with accelerated promotions now (spiritual, ministerial, financial, physical, material, marital, global impact) in the name of Jesus.

20. I receive grace and power to lift me up for Kingdom advancement in the name of Jesus.

21. O Lord, move me to higher heights for Your Kingdom advancement in the name of Jesus.

22. O Lord, establish me, my family, and helpers of my destiny in Your new Kingdom in the name of Jesus.

23. Holy Spirit, You are my encourager, advance my Kingdom assignments gloriously and courageously in the name of Jesus.

24. O Lord, take away all limits with which the enemy has hindered my God ordained vision in the name of Jesus.

25. O Lord, work on me and that which concerns me for Your kingdom advancement in the name of Jesus.

One day Moses said to the LORD, "You have been telling me, 'Take these people up to the Promised Land.' But you haven't told me whom you will send with me. You have told me, 'I know you by name, and I look favorably on you.' If it is true that you look favorably on me, let me know your ways so I may understand you more fully and continue to enjoy your favor. And remember that this nation is your very own people." The LORD replied, "I will personally go with you, Moses, and I will give you rest; everything will be fine for you." Then Moses said, "If you don't personally go with us, don't make us leave this place. How will anyone know that you look favorably on me; on me and on your people; if you don't go with us? For your presence among us sets your people and me apart from all other people on the earth." The LORD replied to Moses, "I will indeed do what you have asked, for I look favorably on you, and I know you by name." Moses responded, "Then show me your glorious presence." The LORD replied, "I will make all my goodness pass before you, and I will call out my name, Yahweh, before you. For I will show mercy to anyone I choose, and I will show compassion to anyone I choose. (Exodus 33:12-19 NLT)

26. O Lord, if I have found grace in Your sight, show me Your glory for Your kingdom advancement in the name of Jesus.

27. O Lord, give me the people You will use with me for the new dispensation of Your kingdom advancement in the name of Jesus.

28. O Lord, show me the way for Your Kingdom advancement in the name of Jesus.

29. O Lord, grant me grace so that Your manifest glorious presence will never depart from me in the name of Jesus.

30. O Lord, give divine rest and comfort in life and ministry in the name of Jesus.

31. O Lord, help me to continually be engaged In Your thoughts and to obey Your word without ceasing in the name of Jesus.

32. O Lord, meet my needs and wants exceeding mightily now in the name of Jesus.

DIVINE SPEED

1. Father, open my eyes to receive what You have for me in wealth creation, in the name of Jesus.

2. Father, take away from my relationship time wasters, in the name of Jesus

3. O Lord, grant unto me excellent spirit in all my life and ministry endeavors in the name of Jesus.

4. Father, empower me for Your use and relevance in the name of Jesus.

5. Father, announce my gifts in a superlative dimension in the name of Jesus.

6. Father, re-brand me in the fullness of Your power, grace, wisdom glory in the name of Jesus.

7. O Lord, lift me up and let me stand on heaven's tableland in the name of Jesus.

8. Father, guide me and lead me to overtake those who have gone ahead of me with good success in the name of Jesus.

9. Father You know my needs and wants, I ask that You supply them exceeding abundantly beyond my expectations, in the name of Jesus.

10. O Lord, lavish Your grace upon me, my family, ministry, destiny and interests in the name of Jesus.

11. O Lord, help me to please You with my household all the days of our lives, in the name of Jesus.

12. O Lord, keep me safe in Your pavilion of love, peace, joy and power, in the name of Jesus.

13. Father, grant unto me Your divine encounter with spectacular results and progress in life and destiny, in the name of Jesus.

14. Jesus, You are the Water of life, refresh me all round. Heal me, bless me and lift me higher in the name of Jesus.

15. Father, help me to align my thoughts with Your thoughts, my will with Your will and my ways with Your ways in the name of Jesus.

16. Jesus , You are the way, show me the path to excel ,to succeed, to be fulfilled and to break forth in this glorious year in the name of Jesus.

17. O Lord, let the fire for divine speed fall upon me in the name of Jesus.

18. Holy Spirit, my comforting Comforter, comfort me on every side, (spiritually, physically, materially, maritally, financially, ministerially, academically, career wise etc) for life in the name of Jesus.

19. O Lord, do something new in my life, family, ministry, destiny and nation in the name of Jesus.

20. O Lord, enlarge my coast with supernatural landmarks that cannot be challenged or contested in the name of Jesus.

TOTAL TRANSFORMATION

1. O Lord, wipe away my tears and turn my darkness into light in Jesus name.

2. O Lord, take away whatever pride that brings about shame, and destruction in me, my family, ministry teams and destiny in the name of Jesus.

3. O Lord, every plan You have purposed for my destiny, execute them now without delay. Let them manifest fully in the name of Jesus.

4. O Lord, that miracle that will announce my lifting, fulfillment of my destiny and reposition me for greatness, give it to me now in the name of Jesus.

5. Father, take all the glory for my achievements accomplishments in my life, business, and ministry in the name of Jesus.

6. O Lord, forgive me all my trespasses, take away the siege and fulfill all Your counsel and prophecies in my life, family, businesses and ministry in the name of Jesus.

7. O Lord, establish my foundations in Your FULNESS: Spiritually, materially, physically, ministerially, maritally, financially, economically, emotionally etc in the name of Jesus.

8. O Lord, fill every part of my being with the passion for your presence in the name of Jesus.

9. O Lord, I decree that from henceforth lead me in the

path of my appointment with greatness ,in the name of Jesus.

10. Father, grant unto me remarkable encounters that will usher me into Your unlimited exploits with proofs in the name of Jesus.

11. O Lord, give unto me a new heart of sacrifice, selfless service and compassion in the name of Jesus.

12. Sanctify me, my spouse, my children and work of my hands in the name of Jesus.

13. O Lord, rebuild the ruins in my life, my family, my assignment, my ministry, my business, my finances etc in the name of Jesus.

14. O Lord, deliver me from whatever the enemy has programmed to use to destroy me, my destiny, my ministry and my family in the name of Jesus.

15. O Lord, transform me for Your glory, in the name of Jesus.

16. Father, there is a place called "my place". Establish me in my place of authority in the name of Jesus.

17. O Lord, connect me with nobles and kings in line with your purpose for my life and destiny, in the name of Jesus.

18. O Lord, help me to serve You with singleness of mind , faithfulness and with honest intentions in the name of Jesus.

19. O Lord, use me as Your prophet of restoration to the nations concerning everything the destroyer has destroyed in the name of Jesus.

20. O Lord, grant me a sensitive heart and spirit in the name of Jesus.

21. Father, deliver me from every ulterior motive and negative intention in the name of Jesus.

22. O Lord, deliver me from everything that will cut my life short in the name of Jesus.

23. I decree in the name of Jesus that I will not labour in vain.

24. Father make me unstoppable in the name of Jesus.

25. Go ahead and thank Him for His faithfulness, mercy, and wonderful works in the name of Jesus.

SUPERNATURAL VISITATION

I want to know Christ and experience the mighty power that raised him from the dead. I want to suffer with him, sharing in his death, so that one way or another I will experience the resurrection from the dead! (Philippians 3:10-11 NLT)

1. O Lord, grant me the benefits of the priceless debt You paid for humanity.

2. O Lord, I want to know You more than this. Help me to continually experience the mighty power that raised You from the dead.

3. O Lord, let everything I touch, manifest "the Midas touch" in the name of Jesus.

4. O Lord, give unto me multifaceted power, wisdom, riches of grace, understanding, and visitation in the name of Jesus.

5. O Lord, let the Rivers of Living water flow out of my belly, my family and ministry etc in the name of Jesus.

6. O Lord, let the Rivers of living water manifest signs, wonders, miracles, healing, wisdom, mercy, strange acts, blessings, benefits and riches of grace in me and through me in the name of Jesus.

7. O Lord, I am thirsty. Let Rivers of living water flow from my heart, in the name of Jesus.

8. O Lord, according to Acts 10:38, anoint me with the Holy Ghost and power to do greater exploits in the name of Jesus.

And the Spirit of the LORD will rest on him; the Spirit of wisdom and understanding, the Spirit of counsel and might, the Spirit of knowledge and the fear of the LORD. He will delight in obeying the LORD. He will not judge by appearance nor make a decision based on hearsay. He will give justice to the poor and make fair decisions for the exploited. The earth will shake at the force of his word, and one breath from his mouth will destroy the wicked. (Isaiah 11:2-4 NLT)

9. O Lord, let Your Spirit rest upon me, (the Spirit of wisdom, understanding, counsel, might, knowledge and the fear of the Lord) in the name of Jesus.
10. O Lord, grant me the grace to delight in obeying You in season and out of season in the name of Jesus.
11. O Lord, help me not to judge by appearance, nor make a decision based on hearsay in the name of Jesus.
12. O Lord, let the earth shake at the force of Your spoken word from my mouth, in the name of Jesus.
13. O Lord, let the Power of God come down without ceasing, in the name of Jesus.
14. O Lord, let the Spirit come down without ceasing in Jesus name.

The earth is the LORD's, and everything in it. The world and all its people belong to him. For he laid the earth's foundation on the seas and built it on the ocean depths. They will receive the LORD's blessing and have a right relationship with God their savior. Such people may seek you and worship in your presence, O God of Jacob. Interlude Open up, ancient gates! Open up, ancient doors, and let the King of glory enter. Who is the King of glory? The LORD, strong and mighty; the LORD, invincible in battle. Open up, ancient gates! Open up, ancient doors, and let the King of glory enter. Who is the King of glory? The LORD of Heaven's Armies he is the King of glory. Interlude (Psalm24:1-2, 5-9 NLT)

15. O Lord, open the gates of my fortunes, in the name of Jesus.

Then Joshua told the people, "Purify yourselves, for tomorrow the LORD will do great wonders among you." (Joshua 3:5 NLT)

16. O Lord, do great wonders in my life, family, ministry etc in the name of Jesus.

Therefore, God elevated him to the place of highest honor and gave him the name above all other names, that at the name of Jesus every knee should bow, in heaven and on earth and under the earth, and every tongue declare that Jesus Christ is Lord, to the glory of God the Father. (Philippians 2:9-11 NLT)

17. Father, let the name of Jesus answer for me without ceasing in the name of Jesus.
18. Father, let the covenant and power in the blood of Jesus answer me without ceasing.
19. Father, elevate me, my spouse, children, ministry, resources and destiny to the place of highest honour in the name of Jesus.
20. O Lord, let every creature and tongue, living and non living be subject to the name of Jesus in my mouth, in the name of Jesus.
21. *"He sent out his word and healed them, snatching them*

from the door of death". (Psalm 107:20 NLT)

The Son radiates God's own glory and expresses the very character of God, and he sustains everything by the mighty power of his command. When he had cleansed us from our sins, he sat down in the place of honor at the right hand of the majestic God in heaven. (Hebrews 1:3 NLT)

It is the same with my word. I send it out, and it always produces fruit. It will accomplish all I want it to, and it will prosper everywhere I send it. (Isaiah 55:11 NLT)

22. O Lord, as Your word is powerful in Your mouth, let it be powerful in my mouth too in the name of Jesus.
23. O Lord, grant unto me and my nuclear family, THE TREASURES You promised, in the name of Jesus.
24. O Lord, grant unto me the door of utterances for Your visitation without ceasing, in the name of Jesus.
25. From henceforth, I will enjoy the ministry of angels that proceed from the presence of God (celestial and human) for life in Jesus name.

God has spoken plainly, and I have heard it many times: Power, O God, belongs to you; (Psalm 62:11 NLT)

But you will receive power when the Holy Spirit comes upon you. And you will be my witnesses, telling people about me everywhere; in Jerusalem, throughout Judea, in Samaria, and to the ends of the earth." (Acts of the Apostles 1:8 NLT)

26. O Lord, power belongs to you. Give unto me Your mighty power, in the name of Jesus.
27. O Lord, endue me afresh as Your witness: locally, nationally, internationally, and globally in the name of Jesus.

28. Despatch Your ministering angels to go bring treasures, resources, money, physical benefits and every good thing of life for me in the name of Jesus.
29. Every one owing me or owing anyone that will help me, Angels go and compel them to pay now in the name of Jesus.
30. Anyone, group or organization holding onto what belongs to me; offerings, first fruits, supports, provisions, cars, lands, houses etc. Angels, compel them to release them to me now in the name of Jesus.
31. Begin to celebrate the goodness and mercy of God at work in your life for answered prayers now in the name of Jesus.

I await your testimonies without delay , in the name of Jesus!

COVENANT OF TERRIFIC AND VIOLENT ANOINTING IN RIGHTEOUSNESS (Observe the Holy communion)

The LORD of Heaven's Armies has sworn this oath: "It will all happen as I have planned. It will be as I have decided. (Isaiah 14:24 NLT)

1. O Lord, swear over me and establish Your will and power in me without delay in the name of Jesus.
2. O Lord, Your thought towards me is for good. Let Your goodness and mercy prevail in all my endeavor in Jesus name.

The LORD replied, "Listen, I am making a covenant with you in the presence of all your people. I will perform miracles that have never been performed anywhere in all the earth or in any nation. And all the people around you will see the power of the LORD the awesome power I will display for you. (Exodus 34:10 NLT)

3.   O Lord, establish Your covenant of wonders that have never been performed anywhere in all the earth or in any nation in me in the name of Jesus.
4.   O Lord, show case Your awesome and violent power through me all the days of my life in the name of Jesus.

"I have found my servant David. I have anointed him with my holy oil. I will steady him with my hand; with my powerful arm I will make him strong. His enemies will not defeat him, nor will the wicked overpower him. I will beat down his adversaries before him and destroy those who hate him. My faithfulness and unfailing love will be with him, and by my authority he will grow in power. I will extend his rule over the sea, his dominion over the rivers. And he will call out to me, 'You are my Father, my God, and the Rock of my salvation.' I will make him my firstborn son, the mightiest king on earth. I will love him and be kind to him forever; my covenant with him will never end. I will preserve an heir for him; his throne will be as endless as the days of heaven. But if his descendants forsake my instructions and fail to obey my regulations, if they do not obey my decrees and fail to keep my commands, then I will punish their sin with the rod, and their disobedience with beating. But I will never stop loving him nor fail to keep my promise to him. No, I will not break my covenant; I will not take back a single word I said. I have sworn an oath to David, and in my holiness I cannot lie: His dynasty will go on forever; his kingdom will endure as the sun." (Psalm 89:20-36 NLT)

5.   O Lord, anoint me with Your Holy oil for terrible,

awesome, unusual strange acts, miracles, signs, wonders, blessings, breakthroughs and results in the name of Jesus.

6. O Lord, steady my destiny with Your powerful hand and make me strong in the name of Jesus.

7. O Lord, let not my enemies defeat me, nor allow the wicked to overpower me in the name of Jesus.

8. O Lord, beat all my adversaries and destroy all those who hate me in the name of Jesus.

9. O Lord, let not Your faithfulness and mercy ever depart from me in the name of Jesus.

10. O Lord, by Your authority, let me grow in unusual power in the name of Jesus.

11. O Lord, extend my rule and reign locally, nationally, internationally and globally in the name of Jesus.

12. O Lord, manifest Your firstborn sonship in me without ceasing in the name of Jesus. ·

13. O Lord, love and be kind to me, my family, my ministry for life in the name of Jesus.

14. O Lord, establish Your irreversible everlasting covenant of power, mercy, dominion and your RICHES OF GRACE -with me and all my interests in the name of Jesus.

15. O Lord, establish Your grace and power in me ,so that You will not stop loving me or stop keeping Your promises in my life and interests in the Jesus name.

16. O Lord, never cease from using me for Your glory in the name of Jesus.

17. O Lord, yield Your mercy and power to me exceeding mightily forever in the name of Jesus.

"Every good gift and every perfect (free, large, full) gift is from above; it comes down from the Father of all [that gives] light, in

[the shining of] Whom there can be no variation (rising or setting) or shadow cast by His turning [as in an eclipse]" *(James 1:17 AMP)*

18. O Lord grant unto me every good and perfect gift in the name of Jesus.
19. O Lord, let the power of the Holy Ghost fall upon Me in the name of Jesus.

John5:19-20,26-27,30
So Jesus explained, "I tell you the truth, the Son can do nothing by himself. He does only what he sees the Father doing. Whatever the Father does, the Son also does. For the Father loves the Son and shows him everything he is doing. In fact, the Father will show him how to do even greater works than healing this man. Then you will truly be astonished.

The Father has life in himself, and he has granted that same life-giving power to his Son. And he has given him authority to judge everyone because he is the Son of Man.

I can do nothing on my own. I judge as God tells me. Therefore, my judgment is just, because I carry out the will of the one who sent me, not my own will. (John 5:19-20, 26-27, 30 NLT)

20. Father reveal to me the secrets of Your awesome power, strange acts, and greater works as You did with Jesus in His earthly ministry in the name of Jesus Christ.
21. Father grant unto me same life giving power and authority as You did with Jesus and the apostles in their earthly ministries in the name of Jesus Christ.
22. Father, grant me the wisdom, grace and power to "HEAR and TO DO " in the name of Jesus.

So Jesus said, "When you have lifted up the Son of Man on the cross, then you will understand that I AM he. I do nothing on my own but say only what the Father taught me. And the one who sent me is with me he has not deserted me. For I always do what pleases him." (John 8:28-29 NLT)

23. Father, help me to please You all the days of my life and destiny in the name of Jesus.
24. O Lord, I pray, never desert me, show that You are with me always in the name of Jesus.
25. Administer the Holy communion to yourself and begin to thank Him for the new covenant established with you.

ALL ROUND GLORIOUS PROGRESS

1. O Lord, rebuild my life by the power of the spoken word.
2. I receive divine announcement in all areas of my life, calling, business, finance etc.
3. O Lord, overturn everything about me for the better in Jesus name.
4. The flood gate of joy, increase, peace, prosperity etc, open unto me in Jesus name.
5. All that is giving me joy will not turn to sorrow for me, my work, my wife, my children, my calling etc in Jesus name.
6. O Lord, redeem my life.
7. O Lord, send help to me from far and near.
8. O Lord, open the door of joy and blessing unto me.
9. I will never be stranded in life in Jesus name.
10. Father make room for me, my spouse, my children, my ministry and my helpers of destiny in Jesus name.
11. Every covering cast over my glory, my breakthrough,

my works and my gift, disappear now in Jesus name.

12. Father, decorate my life with Your blessing.

13. Father, I thank You for changing my turban.

14. The tree of my glory will not dry up, in the name of Jesus.

15. The crack in the wall of my glory be rebuilt, in the name of Jesus.

16. Everything in my life that ought not to die and is dead come alive now, in the name of Jesus.

17. God of creative miracles, use me for Your glory (To perform great miracles)

18. O God of Elijah, let Your fire enter into my spirit, ministry and all that I do in the name of Jesus.

19. O Lord, give me unto me violent anointing like Elisha.

20. Arise O Lord, let all Your enemies in my life, family and destiny be scattered in the name of Jesus.

Begin to dance rigorously. Your victory is hereby made manifest in the name of Jesus.
You will testify!

SHOWERS OF BLESSINGS

"I will bless them and let them live round my sacred hill. There I will bless them with showers of rain when they need it. The trees will bear fruit, the fields will produce crops, and everyone will live in safety on his own land. When I break my people's chains and set them free from those who made them slaves, then they will know that I am the Lord. The heathen nations will not plunder them any more, and the wild animals will not kill and eat them. They will live in safety, and no one will terrify them. I will give them fertile fields and put an end to hunger in the land. The other nations will not sneer at them any more. Everyone

will know that I protect Israel and that they are my people. I, the Sovereign Lord, have spoken. "You, my sheep, the flock that I feed, are my people, and I am your God," says the Sovereign Lord. (Ezekiel 34:26-31 GNB)

1. Father, pour on me the showers of Your blessings, in the name of Jesus.
2. Father, increase my greatness and comfort me on every side. You will make me greater than ever; You will comfort me again.

1 Chronicles 12:22
When David was at Hebron, many trained soldiers joined his army to help make him king in place of Saul, as the Lord had promised.

3. Father, establish Your divine shift in my life in the name of Jesus.
4. Father, establish Your divine shift in my business in the name of Jesus.
5. Father, establish Your divine shift in my ministry in the name of Jesus.
6. Father, grant unto me, a new dimension of Your utterances, in the name of Jesus.
7. Father, use me in diverse ways for Your supernatural exploits, in the name of Jesus.
8. Father, grant unto me, my family, my ministry and helpers "the overtaker's anointing", in the name of Jesus.
9. Father, grant me unlimited grace to hear the inaudible and to see the unseeable.

and my teaching and message were not delivered with skillful words of human wisdom, but with convincing proof of the power of God's Spirit. Your faith, then, does not rest on human wisdom but on God's power.

However, as the scripture says: "What no one ever saw or heard, what no one ever thought could happen, is the very thing God prepared for those who love him." (1 Corinthians 2:4-5,9 GNB)

10. Father, breathe on me afresh, for unspeakable exploits in life and ministry, in the name of Jesus.

Jesus said to them again, "Peace be with you. As the Father sent me, so I send you." Then he breathed on them and said, "Receive the Holy Spirit. (John 20:21-22 GNB)·

11. Father, grant unto me giant strides to attain higher grounds, in the name of Jesus.

When I am lifted up from the earth, I will draw everyone to me." (John 12:32 GNB)

12. Father, take me on Your Eagle's wings for life, in the name of Jesus.

"You saw what I, the Lord, did to the Egyptians and how I carried you as an eagle carries her young on her wings, and brought you here to me. Now, if you will obey me and keep my covenant, you will be my own people. The whole earth is mine, but you will be my chosen people, a people dedicated to me alone, and you will serve me as priests." (Exodus 19:4-6 GNB

13. Father, supply my need and that of my family and ministry according Your riches in Christ Jesus.

"And with all his abundant wealth through Christ Jesus, my God will supply all your needs." (Philippians 4:19 GNB)

14. Father, empower me with Your divine speed in the name of Jesus.
15. Father, empower my family and my ministry with Your divine speed in the name of Jesus.
16. Father, take me on a journey into Your presence in the name of Jesus.

"You will show me the path that leads to life; your presence fills me with joy and brings me pleasure for ever." (Psalms 16:11 GNB)

17. Father, open unto me, my family, my ministry new doors of joy in the name of Jesus.

"I will give him complete authority under the king, the descendant of David. He will have the keys of office; what he opens, no one will shut, and what he shuts, no one will open." (Isaiah 22:22 GNB)

18. Father, unlock unto me the hidden treasures and the riches of Gentiles exceeding mightily, in the name of Jesus.

"The Lord has chosen Cyrus to be king! He has appointed him to conquer nations; he sends him to strip kings of their power; the Lord will open the gates of cities for him. To Cyrus the Lord says, "I myself will prepare your way, leveling mountains and hills. I will break down bronze gates and smash their iron bars. I will give you treasures from dark, secret places; then you will know that I am the Lord, and that the God of Israel has called you by name. I appoint you to help my servant Israel, the people that I have chosen. I have given you great honour, although you do not know me." (Isaiah 45:1-4 GNB)

19. Father, grant unto me landed properties that matter in nations of the world.

"I gave you a land that you had never cultivated and cities that you had not built. Now you are living there and eating grapes from vines that you did not plant, and olives from trees that you did not plant." (Joshua 24:13 GNB)

20. Father, what You did with David, Solomon, Daniel, Jabez and Esther, do them in righteous with me and my family in the name of Jesus.

"That night God appeared to Solomon and asked, "What would you like me to give you?" Solomon answered, "You always showed great love for my father David, and now you have let me succeed him as king. O Lord God, fulfill the promise you made to my father. You have made me king over a people who are so many that they cannot be counted, so give me the wisdom and knowledge I need to rule over them. Otherwise, how would I ever be able to rule this great people of yours?" God replied to Solomon, "You have made the right choice. Instead of asking for wealth or treasure or fame or the death of your enemies or even for long life for yourself, you have asked for wisdom and knowledge so that you can rule my people, over whom I have made you king. I will give you wisdom and knowledge. And in addition, I will give you more wealth, treasure, and fame than any king has ever had before or will ever have again." (2 Chronicles 1:7-12 GNB)

"There was a man named Jabez, who was the most respected member of his family. His mother had given him the name Jabez, because his birth had been very painful. But Jabez prayed to the God of Israel, "Bless me, God, and give me much land. Be with me and keep me from anything evil that might

cause me pain." And God gave him what he prayed for." (1 Chronicles 4:9-10 GNB)

"King David announced to the whole assembly: "My son Solomon is the one whom God has chosen, but he is still young and lacks experience. The work to be done is tremendous, because this is not a palace for people but a temple for the Lord God. I have made every effort to prepare materials for the Temple; gold, silver, bronze, iron, timber, precious stones and gems, stones for mosaics, and quantities of marble. Over and above all this that I have provided, I have given silver and gold from my personal property because of my love for God's Temple. I have given more than a hundred tonnes of the finest gold and almost 240 tonnes of pure silver for decorating the walls of the Temple and for all the objects which the skilled workers are to make. Now who else is willing to give a generous offering to the Lord?" Then the heads of the clans, the officials of the tribes, the commanders of the army, and the administrators of the royal property volunteered to give the following for the work on the Temple: more than 170 tonnes of gold, over 340 tonnes of silver, almost 620 tonnes of bronze, and more than 3,400 tonnes of iron. Those who had precious stones gave them to the temple treasury, which was administered by Jehiel of the Levite clan of Gershon. The people had given willingly to the Lord, and they were happy that so much had been given. King David also was extremely happy." (1 Chronicles 297:1-9 GNB)

"On the third day of her fast Esther put on her royal robes and went and stood in the inner courtyard of the palace, facing the throne room. The king was inside, seated on the royal throne, facing the entrance. When the king saw Queen Esther standing outside, she won his favour, and he held out to her the gold

sceptre. She then came up and touched the tip of it. "What is it, Queen Esther?" the king asked. "Tell me what you want, and you shall have it even if it is half my empire." (Esther 5:1-3 GNB)

"He has unusual ability and is wise and skillful in interpreting dreams, solving riddles, and explaining mysteries; so send for this man Daniel, whom the king named Belteshazzar, and he will tell you what all this means." (Daniel 5:12 GNB)

21. Father, raise help for me, my family and my ministry without delay for life, in the name of Jesus.

"Help us against the enemy; human help is worthless. With God on our side we will win; he will defeat our enemies." (Psalms 108:12-13 GNB)

"Our help comes from the Lord, who made heaven and earth". (Psalms 124:8 GNB)

22. Father, release unto me new dimensions of supernatural wealth creation and exploits, in the name of Jesus.

"My dear friend, I pray that everything may go well with you and that you may be in good health ; as I know you are well in spirit." (3 John 1:2 GNB)

23. Father, enlarge my coast than ever before exceeding greatly in the name of Jesus.

"There was a man named Jabez, who was the most respected member of his family. His mother had given him the name Jabez, because his birth had been very painful. But Jabez prayed to the God of Israel, "Bless me, God, and give me much land. Be with me and keep me from anything evil that might

cause me pain." And God gave him what he prayed for."(1 Chronicles 4:9-10 GNB)

24. Father, open my eyes to see, open my ears to hear like never before in the name of Jesus.

"and my teaching and message were not delivered with skillful words of human wisdom, but with convincing proof of the power of God's Spirit. Your faith, then, does not rest on human wisdom but on God's power. However, as the scripture says: "What no one ever saw or heard, what no one ever thought could happen, is the very thing God prepared for those who love him." (1 Corinthians 2:4-5, 9 GNB)

"Why don't you tear the sky apart and come down? The mountains would see you and shake with fear. They would tremble like water boiling over a hot fire. Come and reveal your power to your enemies, and make the nations tremble at your presence! There was a time when you came and did terrifying things that we did not expect; the mountains saw you and shook with fear. No one has ever seen or heard of a God like you, who does such deeds for those who put their hope in him". (Isaiah 64:1-4 GNB)

25. Father, establish in me, an unprecedented dimension of faith that no creation can contend with in the name of Jesus.

"To have faith is to be sure of the things we hope for, to be certain of the things we cannot see. It was by their faith that people of ancient times won God's approval. It is by faith that we understand that the universe was created by God's word, so that what can be seen was made out of what cannot be seen. It was faith that made Abel offer to God a better sacrifice than

Cain's. Through his faith he won God's approval as a righteous man, because God himself approved of his gifts. By means of his faith Abel still speaks, even though he is dead. It was faith that kept Enoch from dying. Instead, he was taken up to God, and nobody could find him, because God had taken him up. The scripture says that before Enoch was taken up, he had pleased God. No one can please God without faith, for whoever comes to God must have faith that God exists and rewards those who seek him."(Hebrews 11:1-6 GNB)

"As for us, we have this large crowd of witnesses round us. So then, let us rid ourselves of everything that gets in the way, and of the sin which holds on to us so tightly, and let us run with determination the race that lies before us. Let us keep our eyes fixed on Jesus, on whom our faith depends from beginning to end. He did not give up because of the cross! On the contrary, because of the joy that was waiting for him, he thought nothing of the disgrace of dying on the cross, and he is now seated at the right-hand side of God's throne"(Hebrews 12:1-2 GNB)

26. Father, grant unto me grace for supernatural exploits, in the name of Jesus.

"By deceit the king will win the support of those who have already abandoned their religion, but those who follow God will fight back." (Daniel 11:32 GNB)

"Whoever believes and is baptized will be saved; whoever does not believe will be condemned. Believers will be given the power to perform miracles: they will drive out demons in my name; they will speak in strange tongues; if they pick up snakes or drink any poison, they will not be harmed; they will place their hands on sick people, who will get well." (Mark 16 :16-18 GNB)

202

27. Father in the name of Jesus, I ask that You grant unto me, grace to make the mountains to boil like water when I stand to minister any where in this world.

"Why don't you tear the sky apart and come down? The mountains would see you and shake with fear." (Isaiah 64:1 GNB)

28. Father, grant me access to see beyond the now, in the name of Jesus.

The Sovereign Lord never does anything without revealing his plan to his servants, the prophets. (Amos 3:7 GNB)

29. Father, grant unto me angelic assistance without ceasing in the name of Jesus.

"What are the angels, then? They are spirits who serve God and are sent by him to help those who are to receive salvation". (Hebrews 1:14 GNB)

30. Jesus Christ, My Lord, my personal Savior and Master, please let me see You face to face every time .

"Some Greeks were among those who had gone to Jerusalem to worship during the festival. They went to Philip (he was from Bethsaida in Galilee) and said, "Sir, we want to see Jesus." (John 12:20-21 GNB)

31. Father, consecrate me afresh for Your glory and Your use in the name of Jesus.

"He must become more important while I become less important." He who comes from above is greater than all. He who is from the earth belongs to the earth and speaks about earthly matters, but he who comes from heaven is above all".

(John 3:30-31 GNB)

32. Thou God of signs, wonders, strange acts, miracles and mighty acts; I ask that You use me for Your glory globally, in the name of Jesus.

33. O Lord, circumcise my heart so as encounter the deeper dimension of Your sacrificial LOVE in the name of Jesus.

"Create a pure heart in me, O God, and put a new and loyal spirit in me. Do not banish me from your presence; do not take your holy spirit away from me. Give me again the joy that comes from your salvation, and make me willing to obey you." "My sacrifice is a humble spirit, O God; you will not reject a humble and repentant heart. "(Psalm 51 :10-12, 17 GNB)

"As a deer longs for a stream of cool water, so I long for you, O God. I thirst for you, the living God; when can I go and worship in your presence? Day and night I cry, and tears are my only food; all the time my enemies ask me, "Where is your God?" (Psalm 42 :1-3 GNB)

"O God, you are my God, and I long for you. My whole being desires you; like a dry, worn-out, and waterless land, my soul is thirsty for you. Let me see you in the sanctuary; let me see how mighty and glorious you are. Your constant love is better than life itself, and so I will praise you. I will give you thanks as long as I live; I will raise my hands to you in prayer. My soul will feast and be satisfied, and I will sing glad songs of praise to you." (Psalm 63:1-5 GNB)

34. Father, baptize me afresh with Your Holy Spirit in the name of Jesus.

"But when the Holy Spirit comes upon you, you will be filled

with power, and you will be witnesses for me in Jerusalem, in all Judea and Samaria, and to the ends of the earth." (Acts 1:8 GNB)

"You know about Jesus of Nazareth and how God poured out on him the Holy Spirit and power. He went everywhere, doing good and healing all who were under the power of the Devil, for God was with him". (Acts 10:38 GNB)

35. O Lord, take me to the deeper and greater height of Your supernatural exploits, favors, provisions and benefits of Grace and mercy in the name of Jesus.

"They grow stronger as they go; they will see the God of gods on Zion. The Lord is our protector and glorious king, blessing us with kindness and honour. He does not refuse any good thing to those who do what is right." (Psalm 84:7, 11 GNB)

36. Father, use me as an instrument of Your wonders, strange acts, wonders, miracles and blessings in the name of Jesus.

"I will give you the keys of the Kingdom of heaven; what you prohibit on earth will be prohibited in heaven, and what you permit on earth will be permitted in heaven." (Matthew 16:19 GNB

"And so I tell all of you: what you prohibit on earth will be prohibited in heaven, and what you permit on earth will be permitted in heaven." (Matthew 18:18 GNB)

"For forty days after his death he appeared to them many times in ways that proved beyond doubt that he was alive. They saw him, and he talked with them about the Kingdom of God." (Acts 1:3 GNB)

37. Father, recreate me anew for Your glory in the name of Jesus.

"Anyone who is joined to Christ is a new being; the old is gone, the new has come." (2 Corinthians 5:17 GNB)

38. Endow and empower me with the fullness of Your grace and power, in the name of Jesus.

"Out of the fullness of his grace he has blessed us all, giving us one blessing after another." (John 1:16 GNB)

"Out of the fullness of his grace he has blessed us all, giving us one blessing after another." (John 1:16 GNB)

39. Holy Ghost, baptize me with grace for divine ease and proofs in the name of Jesus.

"When the day of Pentecost came, all the believers were gathered together in one place. Suddenly there was a noise from the sky which sounded like a strong wind blowing, and it filled the whole house where they were sitting. Then they saw what looked like tongues of fire which spread out and touched each person there. They were all filled with the Holy Spirit and began to talk in other languages, as the Spirit enabled them to speak."(Acts 2:1-4 GNB)

"With great power the apostles gave witness to the resurrection of the Lord Jesus, and God poured rich blessings on them all" (Acts 4:33 GNB)

40. Father, I ask in the name of Jesus that You send down (Holy Ghost) fire upon me, family, ministry, and the works of my hands in the name of Jesus.

"When the day of Pentecost came, all the believers were gathered together in one place. Suddenly there was a noise from the sky which sounded like a strong wind blowing, and it filled the whole house where they were sitting. Then they saw what looked like tongues of fire which spread out and touched each person there. They were all filled with the Holy Spirit and began to talk in other languages, as the Spirit enabled them to speak." (Acts 2:1-4 GNB)

"But when the Holy Spirit comes upon you, you will be filled with power, and you will be witnesses for me in Jerusalem, in all Judea and Samaria, and to the ends of the earth." (Acts 1:8 GNB)

"With great power the apostles gave witness to the resurrection of the Lord Jesus, and God poured rich blessings on them all." (Acts 4:33 DGNB)

41. Father, transform me from a noise to a voice in the name of Jesus.

"Six days later Jesus took with him Peter and the brothers James and John and led them up a high mountain where they were alone. As they looked on, a change came over Jesus: his face was shining like the sun, and his clothes were dazzling white. Then the three disciples saw Moses and Elijah talking with Jesus. So Peter spoke up and said to Jesus, "Lord, how good it is that we are here! If you wish, I will make three tents here, one for you, one for Moses, and one for Elijah." While he was talking, a shining cloud came over them, and a voice from the cloud said, "This is my own dear Son, with whom I am pleased listen to him!" (Matthew 17:1-5 GNB)

42. Father, let the rain of Your power flood my spirit, my

soul and my body in the name of Jesus.

"From east to west everyone will fear him and his great power. He will come like a rushing river, like a strong wind." (Isaiah 59:19 GNB)

43. Thank God for answered prayers.

CROWNING THE YEAR WITH HIS GOODNESS

"You crown the year with Your goodness, And Your paths drip with abundance." (Psalm 65:11 NKJV)

1. Father, thank You for crowning the year for me with Your goodness in the name of Jesus.
2. Father, thank You for granting me abundance of all good things in the name of Jesus.

"And the patriarchs, becoming envious, sold Joseph into Egypt. But God was with him and delivered him out of all his troubles, and gave him favor and wisdom in the presence of Pharaoh, king of Egypt; and he made him governor over Egypt and all his house." (Acts 7:9-10 NKJV)

3. Father, thank You for always being with me, my family, my works and my nation in the name of Jesus.
4. Father, deliver me, my family, ministry, and nation from all our troubles (spiritual, ministerial, financial, material, marital, paternal, maternal, emotional, numerical, physical, social, mental, academical) in the name of Jesus.
5. Father, grant us favour and wisdom before all and sundry in Jesus name.

"Therefore they stayed there a long time, speaking boldly in the Lord, who was bearing witness to the word of His grace,

granting signs and wonders to be done by their hands." (Acts 14:3 NKJV)

6. Father, grant me the grace to speak boldly continually without ceasing by adding testimonies to Your word of grace in the name of Jesus.
7. Father, bear witness to Your word of grace without ceasing in the name of Jesus.
8. Father, grant unto me that signs and wonders be done by my hands in the name of Jesus.

"Let God arise, Let His enemies be scattered; Let those also who hate Him flee before Him. As smoke is driven away, So drive them away; As wax melts before the fire, So let the wicked perish at the presence of God. But let the righteous be glad; Let them rejoice before God; Yes, let them rejoice exceedingly." (Psalm 68:1-3 NKJV)

9. Father, arise in my favour and let all Your enemies be scattered in the name of Jesus.
10. Father, let all those who hate You flee from Your presence in the name of Jesus.
11. Father, help me to rejoice before You exceedingly without ceasing in the name of Jesus.

"Through the LORD's mercies we are not consumed, Because His compassions fail not. They are new every morning; Great is Your faithfulness"(Lamentations 3:22-23 NKJV)

12. Father, release over me, my family, ministry and nation, Your mercy without ceasing in the name of Jesus.
13. Father, grant unto me the compassionate heart, nature, and STRENGTH of Jesus Christ.
14. Father, manifest the FULNESS of Your faithfulness in

my life, family, ministry and   nation in the name of Jesus.

15. Father, I ask for the newness of Your mercies and faithfulness that are new every morning in the name of Jesus.

16. Father, grant unto me greater than Your sure mercy of David in the name of Jesus.

17. Father, crown my year and that of my family members, helpers and messengers of joy with Your goodness , proofs, and blessings exceedingly in the name of Jesus.

"David therefore departed from there and escaped to the cave of Adullam. So when his brothers and all his father's house heard it, they went down there to him. And everyone who was in distress, everyone who was in debt, and everyone who was discontented gathered to him. So he became captain over them. And there were about four hundred men with him. Then David went from there to Mizpah of Moab; and he said to the king of Moab, "Please let my father and mother come here with you, till I know what God will do for me." So he brought them before the king of Moab, and they dwelt with him all the time that David was in the stronghold. Now the prophet Gad said to David, "Do not stay in the stronghold; depart, and go to the land of Judah." So David departed and went into the forest of Hereth." (I Samuel 22:1-5 NKJV

18. Father, visit me and all my helpers with Your presence for total victorious testimonies in the name of Jesus.

19. Father deliver me from all my distress, indebtedness discontentment (spiritual, ministerial, financial, material, marital, biological, physical, emotional, mental, health wise, career wise e.t.c. In Jesus name.

20. Father, deliver me from all my weaknesses and limitations (spiritual, financial, numerical, marital, emotional, known and unknown) in the name of Jesus.

21. Father, open my eyes as an individual, family, career person to see and know Your will at all times in the name of Jesus.

22. Father, deliver me from every stronghold and take me to my land of praise in the name of Jesus.

23. Father, use me the more in such an unprecedented way than I have ever encountered in the name of Jesus.

24. Father, supply all my needs according to Your riches in glory by Christ Jesus. *(Philippians 4:14-19).*

25. Father, birth many more new things for me, through me, through my family, through Your church now in the name of Jesus.

26. Father, birth new songs, new anointing, new joy, new grace, new moves through me and mine in the name of Jesus.

27. Father, turnaround my situations, circumstances conditions for the better in the name of Jesus. *(Ezekiel 21:27).*

28. Father, arise fight for me in a way no man can do in the name of Jesus. *(Psalm 68:1-3)*

"And Jesus increased in wisdom and stature, and in favor with God and men". (Luke 2:52 NKJV)

29. Father, grant me increased wisdom and long life in the name of Jesus.

30. Father, grant me increased favour with You and men in the name of Jesus.

31. Father, restore unto me whatever good thing that I have lost in the name of Jesus.

32. Father, contend with forces contending with me, my family, my career, Your church and nation in the name of Jesus.

33. Father, do something outstandingly unique for the better in me, my family, Your church and nation in the name of Jesus.

34. Father, scatter all those who are scheming for me to loose my rewards in the name of Jesus.

"There are also celestial bodies and terrestrial bodies; but the glory of the celestial is one, and the glory of the terrestrial is another. There is one glory of the sun, another glory of the moon, and another glory of the stars; for one star differs from another star in glory." (I Corinthians 15:40-41 NKJV

35. Father, grant unto me Your exceeding surpassing glory and let it shine without struggles in the name of Jesus.

"The thief does not come except to steal, and to kill, and to destroy. I have come that they may have life, and that they may have it more abundantly." (John 10:10 NKJV)

36. I bind you devil and your cohort! You will not steal ,kill and destroy in my family, in the church of God and all my interests in the name of Jesus.

37. I decree that the rod of wickedness will not rest upon any of my interests in the name of Jesus.

38. I sanctify myself and my household with the blood of Jesus. There shall be no loss in the name of Jesus.

39. Father, let my gifts begin to make room for me in the name of Jesus. *(Proverbs 16:18).*

40. Father, grant unto me higher dimensions of Your experience (life, ministry, resources, treasures , encounters, proofs, accomplishments, signs, wonders,

strange acts, miracles, settlements, favour etcetera) in the name of Jesus.

41. Whatever stronghold that I have been carrying over; be it from my father's house, my mother's house, be it from my in law's house, be destroyed in the name of Jesus.

42. I decree that there shall be no loss in my family in the name of Jesus.

"Are they not all ministering spirits sent forth to minister for those who will inherit salvation?"(Hebrews 1:14 NKJV

43. Father, let Your ministering spirits and my guardian angels be active for my profiting (in ministry, business, marriage, health, safety, security, finance, favour, blessing etcetera) in the name of Jesus.

44. Father, let it be that every thing that I touch prospers in the name of Jesus.

"You will arise and have mercy on Zion; For the time to favor her, Yes, the set time, has come." (Psalm 102:13 NKJV)

45. Father, manifest the FULNESS of Your favour in my life, family, business, and Your church in the name of Jesus.

46. Father, be no more silent concerning my matter, ARISE O Lord, favour me and show me Your MERCY in the name of Jesus. *(Judges 15:1-15)*

47. I command every Goliath in my life, my family, my career, and Your church to die now in the name of Jesus. *(1 Sam 17:1-51)*

48. Father, whatever might have been despising Your glory, purpose and authority in my life, my family, my career, Your church and nations, die now in the name of Jesus.

49. You forces challenging my God ordained prophetic

agenda, judgement is upon you now! Die in the name of Jesus.

50. Father, favour me and show me Your mercy with outstanding testimonies, in the name of Jesus.

51. Whatever might have been defiling me and all my interests, die now in the name of Jesus.

52. Father, grant unto me a mouth and wisdom to subdue, dominate and reign even in the midst of my enemies in the name of Jesus. *(Luke 21:15; Rev 5:10)*

53. Father, favour me and show me mercy as Your living proof in the name of Jesus. *(Rev 5:12)*

54. Father, do something peculiar in my life, family and Your church, that only Your favour and mercy can do in the name of Jesus. *(1 Corinthians 2:9).*

55. You devouring wasters of my vineyard, you are a liar! Die now in the name of Jesus.

56. Any creature; animate or inanimate that is working against my comfort, inheritance and settlements, you are a lie, die now in the name of Jesus.

"The LORD brings the counsel of the nations to nothing; He makes the plans of the peoples of no effect. The counsel of the LORD stands forever, The plans of His heart to all generations". (Psalm 33:10-11 NKJV)

57. Father, make the counsel of the wicked against me, my family, Your church and nation to be null and void in the name of Jesus.

58. Father, let only Your counsel for my destiny, that of my family, Your church and nation stand forever in the name of Jesus.

NOW MAKE YOUR PERSONAL REQUESTS KNOWN TO GOD.

GROWING IN GRACE

"May you be made strong with all the strength which comes from his glorious power, so that you may be able to endure everything with patience. And with joy give thanks to the Father, who has made you fit to have your share of what God has reserved for his people in the kingdom of light." (Colossians 1:11-12 GNT)

"But continue to grow in the grace and knowledge of our Lord and Savior Jesus Christ. To him be the glory, now and forever! Amen. "(2 Peter 3:18 GNT)

1. Every enemy of Grace in my life, be uprooted in Jesus name. Let there be a higher unction of GRACE.

"For I am the least of the apostles, who am not worthy to be called an apostle, because I persecuted the church of God. But by the grace of God I am what I am, and His grace toward me was not in vain; but I labored more abundantly than they all, yet not I, but the grace of God which was with me". (I Corinthians 15:9-10 NKJV)

2. Let Your grace give me a lift that will shock the world. Bring me into the elevator of Your Grace.

"I thank my God always on your behalf, for the grace of God which is given you by Jesus Christ; That in every thing ye are enriched by him, in all utterance, and in all knowledge; Even as the testimony of Christ was confirmed in you: So that ye come behind in no gift; waiting for the coming of our Lord Jesus Christ: Who shall also confirm you unto the end, that ye may be blameless in the day of our Lord Jesus Christ." (1 Corinthians

1:4-8 KJV)

"So they shall put My name on the children of Israel, and I will bless them." (Numbers 6:27 NKJV)

"Now when they saw the boldness and unfettered eloquence of Peter and John and perceived that they were unlearned and untrained in the schools [common men with no educational advantages], they marveled; and they recognized that they had been with Jesus". (Acts 4:13 AMP)

3. As a carrier of the name of God, let strange proofs be made manifest in my life and ministry in the name of Jesus.
4. Every mark of the enemy speaking against me and my ministry, be wiped away, in the name of Jesus.

"From now on let no person trouble me (by making it necessary for me to vindicate my apostolic authority and the divine truth of my Gospel), for I bear on my body the (brand) marks of the Lord Jesus (the wounds, scars, and other outward evidence of persecutions; these testify to His ownership of me)" (Galatians 6:17 AMP)

"(But) to this day I have had the help which comes from God (as my ally), and so I stand here testifying to small and great alike, asserting nothing beyond what the prophets and Moses declared would come to pass. (Acts 26:22 AMP)

O Lord! Restore our cutting edge in evangelism and witnessing, in the name of Jesus.

The passion upon Jesus for soul winning, come upon us, in the name of Jesus.

Every man is an architect of the help he receives from the Lord."

"Let Reuben live, and not die; and let not his men be few."
(Deuteronomy 33:6 KJV)

5. My ministry must live and not die in the name of Jesus. I must Excel, Lord! My men shall not be few.

"And this is the blessing of Judah: and he said, Hear, Lord, the voice of Judah, and bring him unto his people: let his hands be sufficient for him; and be thou an help to him from his enemies". (Deuteronomy 33:7 KJV)

6 a. Lord! Hear my voice. *(Isaiah 65:24; Psalm 62:11; Matt 7:7-11)*

   b. Let my hand be sufficient for me, in the name of Jesus.

   c. This hand of mine will not be barren, in the name of Jesus.

   d. Lord, be thou my help from my enemies, in the name of Jesus.

"And it came to pass, as we went to prayer, a certain damsel possessed with a spirit of divination met us, which brought her masters much gain by soothsaying: The same followed Paul and us, and cried, saying, These men are the servants of the most high God, which shew unto us the way of salvation. And this did she many days. But Paul, being grieved, turned and said to the spirit, I command thee in the name of Jesus Christ to come out of her. And he came out the same hour". (Acts 16:16-18 KJV)

7. Any spirit of deception, stagnation, discomfort, reproach, ungodly relationships that I have nurtured over the years, be wasted (the blood of Jesus is against you) in the name of Jesus.

"And a certain man lame from his mother's womb was carried, whom they laid daily at the gate of the temple which is called Beautiful, to ask alms of them that entered into the temple; Who seeing Peter and John about to go into the temple asked an alms. And Peter, fastening his eyes upon him with John, said, Look on us. And he gave heed unto them, expecting to receive something of them. Then Peter said, Silver and gold have I none; but such as I have give I thee: In the name of Jesus Christ of Nazareth rise up and walk. And he took him by the right hand, and lifted him up: and immediately his feet and ankle bones received strength. And he leaping up stood, and walked, and entered with them into the temple, walking, and leaping, and praising God. And all the people saw him walking and praising God" (Acts 3:2-9 KJV)

8. Every spirit of lameness that has kept me on the same spot, I curse you to die in my life, in my ministry, in my business etc.

9. I am graced and blessed to enter a new dimension of grace and power; to enter into that big league. I refuse to live at the mercy of men. I am entering into my ordained placements in the name of Jesus.

"And he saith unto them, Draw out now, and bear unto the governor of the feast. And they bare it. When the ruler of the feast had tasted the water that was made wine, and knew not whence it was: (but the servants which drew the water knew;) the governor of the feast called the bridegroom, And saith unto him, Every man at the beginning doth set forth good wine; and when men have well drunk, then that which is worse: but thou hast kept the good wine until now". (John 2:8-10 KJV)

10. That good thing the Lord has kept for me till now must

show up now, in the name of Jesus.

"Now therefore, I pray thee, if I have found grace in thy sight, shew me now thy way, that I may know thee, that I may find grace in thy sight: and consider that this nation is thy people. And he said, My presence shall go with thee, and I will give thee rest. And he said unto him, If thy presence go not with me, carry us not up hence." (Exodus 33:13-15 KJV)

11. Lord, Grant me rest, in the name of Jesus.

"But ye shall receive power, after that the Holy Ghost is come upon you: and ye shall be witnesses unto me both in Jerusalem, and in all Judaea, and in Samaria, and unto the uttermost part of the earth." (Acts 1:8 KJV)

12. Lord, Empower me with Your power that is irresistible: that satan, demons, poverty, marine powers etc cannot resist, or confront in the name of Jesus.

"And my speech and my preaching was not with enticing words of man's wisdom, but in demonstration of the Spirit and of power: That your faith should not stand in the wisdom of men, but in the power of God." (1 Corinthians 2:4-5 KJV)

13. Father, Manifest Your power in my life, ministry, business etc, in the name of Jesus. I come against the spirit of "the emptier", and I command it to catch fire, in the name of Jesus.
    * By Your mercy Lord, repair my life.
    * Repair my prayer altar.
    * Repair my treasures.
    * Repair my glory.
    * Repair my career.
    * Repair the works of my hand.

* Repair my destiny.
* Repair my body.
* Repair my finances.
* O Lord! By Your mercy, repair me Lord.
* Repair my honour in the name of Jesus.
* Repair my garment of honour in the name of Jesus.
* Repair my commitment, in the name of Jesus.
* Repair my obedience, in the name of Jesus.

14. O Lord! Open the path of good things for me, in the name of Jesus.

15. As long as the wind cannot be blocked, my destiny and my breakthrough shall not be blocked, in the name of Jesus.

16. O Lord, cause men to celebrate me. I will not be left out. Let my ministry be celebrated in the name of Jesus. From henceforth let there be supernatural celebration in Your churches, ministries etc. Father! Let my family be celebrated, in the name of Jesus.

"And Jesus increased in wisdom and stature, and in favour with God and man". (Luke 2:52 KJV)

17. Lord, baptize me with Your favour. Make me Your favour magnet on a daily basis, in the name of Jesus.

"And David said, Is there yet any that is left of the house of Saul, that I may shew him kindness for Jonathan's sake?" (2 Samuel 9:1 KJV)

Favor brings restoration. Lord! Favour me for the next level, in the name of Jesus. Somebody must show me kindness, in the name of Jesus.

18. O Lord, cease the sleep of anyone that You have

ordained to take me to my next level; until he/she releases my next level, in the name of Jesus.

* They will not carry my next level to another place, in the name of Jesus.
* Messengers of my testimonies, come forth now in the name of Jesus.

"For God is not unrighteous to forget your work and labour of love, which ye have shewed toward his name, in that ye have ministered to the saints, and do minister. (Hebrews 6:10 KJV) Father! Your grace upon my life will not be in vain."

"Until the spirit be poured upon us from on high, and the wilderness be a fruitful field, and the fruitful field be counted for a forest". (Isaiah 32:15 KJV)

19. Let Your grace upon my life be productive. Help me not to receive your grace in vain. I will be productive (fruitful) with Your grace.

"Henceforth I call you not servants; for the servant knoweth not what his lord doeth: but I have called you friends; for all things that I have heard of my Father I have made known unto you. Ye have not chosen me, but I have chosen you, and ordained you, that ye should go and bring forth fruit, and that your fruit should remain: that whatsoever ye shall ask of the Father in my name, he may give it you. (John 15:15-16 KJV)

My ordination (Grace released upon my life) will not be wasted, in the name of Jesus."

"They know not, neither will they understand; they walk in darkness: all the foundations of the earth are out of course." (Psalm 82:5 KJV)

20. Lord, open my eyes of understanding. Make them clear in Jesus name.

"That the God of our Lord Jesus Christ, the Father of glory, may give unto you the spirit of wisdom and revelation in the knowledge of him: The eyes of your understanding being enlightened; that ye may know what is the hope of his calling, and what the riches of the glory of his inheritance in the saints, And what is the exceeding greatness of his power to us-ward who believe, according to the working of his mighty power, Which he wrought in Christ, when he raised him from the dead, and set him at his own right hand in the heavenly places, Far above all principality, and power, and might, and dominion, and every name that is named, not only in this world, but also in that which is to come: And hath put all things under his feet, and gave him to be the head over all things to the church, Which is his body, the fulness of him that filleth all in all". (Ephesians 1:17-23 KJV)

"Through wisdom is an house builded; and by understanding it is established: And by knowledge shall the chambers be filled with all precious and pleasant riches. A wise man is strong; yea, a man of knowledge increaseth strength. (Proverbs 24:3-5 KJV)

21. In any way I have been running without understanding, O Lord, straighten me up for Your glory, in the name of Jesus. Lord, whatever understanding I need to get for my fulfillment, give it to me with speed."

22. Grant me understanding of my calling and purpose, in the name of Jesus.

"But there is a spirit in man: and the inspiration of the Almighty giveth them understanding." (Job 32:8 KJV)

23. Lord, let my spirit man be quickened unto understanding. O Lord, upgrade my understanding in life ministry, in the name of Jesus.
24. In any area of my life and ministry that I have been walking in darkness, let Your light flood my darkness, in the name of Jesus.

And I went up by revelation, and communicated unto them that gospel which I preach among the Gentiles, but privately to them which were of reputation, lest by any means I should run, or had run, in vain. (Galatians 2:2 KJV)

25. Lord, make Your plans for me this year clearer, in the name of Jesus. Lord, help me, I don't want to walk in darkness concerning any of my life, the church and ministry.
26. Grant me the grace to be obedient. Where my understanding is obsolete, O Lord, upgrade me.

GENERAL THANKSGIVING

1. Thank God for your life, family, career, projects etc.

"And give thanks for everything to God the Father in the name of our Lord Jesus Christ." (Ephesians 5:20 NLT)

2. Father I thank You for the life of goodness that I am enjoying in the name of Jesus.
3. Father, thank You for my all round settlement in the name of Jesus.

"You will succeed in whatever you choose to do, and light will shine on the road ahead of you. If people are in trouble and you say, 'Help them,' God will save them. Even sinners will be rescued; they will be rescued because your hands are pure." (Job

4. Father, thank You for all the sacrifices you paid for my salvation in the name of Jesus.

5. Thank God for every member of your family (nuclear and extended) in the name of Jesus.

"But if you refuse to serve the LORD, then choose today whom you will serve. Would you prefer the gods your ancestors served beyond the Euphrates? Or will it be the gods of the Amorites in whose land you now live? But as for me and my family, we will serve the LORD." (Joshua 24:15 NLT)

6. Thank You for new revelations of Your MERCY in me, my family, Your church, works, finances, and destiny in the name of Jesus.

7. Father, thank You for Your goodness and mercy every day of my life in the name of Jesus.

8. Father, thank You for new manifestations of your glorious grace, power, wonders, testimonies in and through my life, family, career, Your church, etc in the name of Jesus.

9. O Lord, thank You for the effectiveness of Your word in my mouth, life and career in the name of Jesus.

10. Thank You Lord for new dimensions of unusual, creative, violent grace and power that cannot be insulted, resisted, confronted, abused or shamed, in the name Jesus.

11. Father thank You for the dynamics of Your miraculous, strange acts, marvels, spiritual gifts, ministry gifts in my life, my family, Your church, ministries in the name of Jesus.

12. Father, thank You for the new dreams, new visions, new results and new speed in the name of Jesus.

13. O Lord, thank You for the new wonders; for the cure of incurable diseases through me in the name of Jesus.

"For God's gifts and his call can never be withdrawn." *(Romans 11:29*

14. O Lord, I thank You for the expansion of Your church, treasures, ministries, businesses, impacts on all front without ceasing in the name of Jesus.
15. Thank You Lord for all You are doing in my life, family, ministry, and Your church in the name of Jesus.
16. Father thank you for enlarging my coast (spiritually, physically, financially, economically, mentally, ministerially, emotionally, materially) in the name of Jesus.

"There was a man named Jabez who was more honorable than any of his brothers. His mother named him Jabez because his birth had been so painful. He was the one who prayed to the God of Israel, "Oh, that you would bless me and expand my territory! Please be with me in all that I do, and keep me from all trouble and pain!" And God granted him his request. (1 Chronicles 4:9-10 NLT)

"This is what the LORD says to Cyrus, his anointed one, whose right hand he will empower. Before him, mighty kings will be paralyzed with fear. Their fortress gates will be opened, never to shut again. This is what the LORD says: "I will go before you, Cyrus, and level the mountains. I will smash down gates of bronze and cut through bars of iron. And I will give you treasures hidden in the darkness; secret riches. I will do this so you may know that I am the LORD, the God of Israel, the one who calls you by name. "And why have I called you for this work? Why did I call you by name when you did not know me?

It is for the sake of Jacob my servant, Israel my chosen one. I am the LORD; there is no other God. I have equipped you for battle, though you don't even know me, so all the world from east to west will know there is no other God. I am the LORD, and there is no other. I create the light and make the darkness. I send good times and bad times. I, the LORD, am the one who does these things. "Open up, O heavens, and pour out your righteousness. Let the earth open wide so salvation and righteousness can sprout up together. I, the LORD, created them."(Isaiah 45:1-8 NLT)

17. Father thank You for Your love for me ,my family, ministry, destiny, treasures in the name of Jesus.

"For this is how God loved the world: He gave his one and only Son, so that everyone who believes in him will not perish but have eternal life. God sent his Son into the world not to judge the world, but to save the world through him. "There is no judgment against anyone who believes in him. But anyone who does not believe in him has already been judged for not believing in God's one and only Son. And the judgment is based on this fact: God's light came into the world, but people loved the darkness more than the light, for their actions were evil. All who do evil hate the light and refuse to go near it for fear their sins will be exposed. But those who do what is right come to the light so others can see that they are doing what God wants." (John 3:16-21 NLT)

18. O Lord, thank You for the fresh oil upon my head, that of my spouse and children in the name of Jesus.
19. Father, thank You for using me in Your unprecedented ways in the name of Jesus.
20. Father, thank You for unusual boldness and victories in

the name of Jesus.

21. Father, thank You for empowering me as a savior in Jesus name.

"Then saviors shall come to Mount Zion To judge the mountains of Esau, And the kingdom shall be the LORD's" (Obadiah 1:21 NKJV)

22. My Friend, Comforter, Counsellor, Helper, Intercessor, Advocate, Teacher, my Paraclete, Strengthener and Standby thank You for who You are (in and to me).

"But when the Father sends the Advocate as my representative that is, the Holy Spirit he will teach you everything and will remind you of everything I have told you". (John 14:26 NLT)

23. Father, thank You for the new heights, new depths, new lengths, new breadth of Your provisions, authority and power in my life family, my business, my ministry and outreaches in the name of Jesus.

24. O Lord, I thank You for the "gift of on time" in the name of Jesus.

"No longer will babies die when only a few days old. No longer will adults die before they have lived a full life. No longer will people be considered old at one hundred! Only the cursed will die that young! In those days people will live in the houses they build and eat the fruit of their own vineyards. Unlike the past, invaders will not take their houses and confiscate their vineyards. For my people will live as long as trees, and my chosen ones will have time to enjoy their hard-won gains. They will not work in vain, and their children will not be doomed to misfortune. For they are people blessed by the LORD, and their

children, too, will be blessed. I will answer them before they even call to me. While they are still talking about their needs, I will go ahead and answer their prayers!" (Isaiah 65:20-24 NLT)

25. Father, thank You for Your mighty miracles, signs, wonders, healing, settlement etc in the name of Jesus.
26. O Lord, I thank You For for granting unto me the "Killer's anointing" to put an end to contrary forces in the name of Jesus.
27. O Lord, I thank You for Your triumphant entry into our affairs, families, churches, ministries, finances, businesses, safety, victory, healing, deliverance, etc in the name of Jesus.

Thank You Jesus for answered prayers.

Thank You for settling me in every area.

I give You praise and glory!

BOOKS BY AFOLABI SAMUEL COKER

A PERSONAL PRAYER GUIDE

This book incorporates scriptural prayer points on every facet of life. It also includes positive confessional statements that will turn ordinary people into dynamic Christians.

DON'T CALL IT QUITS

Will reawaken in the readers, all their dead hopes and aspirations. It is a must read for all those who are going through hopeless situations.

EARLY MORNING SETTLEMENT PRAYER #1

This book will equip you to seek the face of the Lord early in the morning when there is no distraction. The wonderful testimonies therein highlight the power of God to answer prayers as of old. Equip yourself with this treasure and you will not be disappointed.

EARLY MORNING SETTLEMENT PRAYER # 2

This will teach you to pray effectively and fervently to get your results. It is sequel to the series #1 edition, and contains prayer points and scriptures in the following areas: Divine Healing, Protection, Deliverance, Marital Delay, No More Bareness. Equip yourself with this treasure and you will be encouraged.

LIVING FOR GOD

Will help you to live for God after you have discovered your identity and purpose through a close relationship with Him. The almighty delights in your selfless service, make up your mind today to live for Him.

GOD'S PROPHETIC AGENDA FOR YOU

"Life without a blue print is like a boat on a sea without a compass. Such is likely to be tossed about by the waves of the sea"

God's prophetic agenda for you outlines the demands of a Christian in his bid to succeed against the seemingly prevailing odds. It highlights what God has purposed prophetically for us and what we ought to do in our endless bid to enhance prosperity, good health and general welfare.

SETTLE ME O LORD

Highlights the need to cry out desperately to God for a settlement, just like Jabez did. He needed more from God than what he had before. When you realize the predicament you are in, and discover the way out, and of course you do what is required of you, God will move on your behalf to settle you.

Enjoy this book, and apply the principles therein; your testimonies will be OUTSTANDING.

MENTOR AND PROTÉGÉ

The content of this book will help you to develop a more meaningful and result-oriented relationship with your subordinates and seniors. It will also help you to make better use of your time, reproduce yourself in others, and help while you are facing the challenges of mentoring or being mentored.

THERE SHALL BE SHOWERS OF BLESSINGS

This book will open your eyes to the blessings of God and how you can position yourself to receive the showers of blessings without measure.

MARITAL MATTERS

The matter of marriage is very important to God and to everyone. MARITAL MATTERS shed a great light on the meaning of marriage and the steps to take to achieve marital success. The book highlights the roles of the husband and the wife and also identifies some challenges that could be encountered and their solutions. The family prayer points in the book will also further establish or strengthen family altar. It is recommended for everyone who desires good marriage, marriage counselors, teachers of the word and parents.

DYNAMICS OF SPIRITUAL LEADERSHIP

This book is a practical guide to successful spiritual leadership. As a duty, every spiritual leader who desires effectiveness and excellent results must learn about the principles underpinning spiritual leadership. A journey through this book will expose you to the tangible principles expressed in simple language for easy understanding. This book will further enhance your knowledge of who you are and also help you to differentiate between VISION and AMBITION. It is highly recommended for everyone called to the responsibility of leadership and all children of God who desire to serve God better.

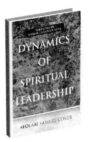

UNTIE THE KNOTTINESS

The need to fulfill God's purpose can not be over emphasized. We need to enhance our fruitfulness and productivity here on earth, so we have to be mindful of the character of Christ in us. This book will help you deal with the limitations, boundaries, and barriers against your God ordained purpose on earth. You are destined to excel in flying colours, so you have to rise up to deal with the "little foxes" and let your vine yield forth it's fruits to full capacity.

A PERSONAL PRAYER GUIDE (YORUBA)

This book is a collection of prayers in Yoruba language.

BOOKS BY ADETUTU OMOLOLA COKER

I'M TOO LOADED TO FAIL

Comprises a 31 day positive confessions for Victorious Living. It will help the children of God to prophesy good about their lives and future on a daily basis. The various topics compiled therein are powerful self-impartations that will turn the reader's life around for good.

I DESIRE TO BE MARRIED

This book is specially inspired by the Spirit of God to give a blue print to those who desire to be married.

I'M DESTINED TO WIN!

Is a powerful book that everyone who desires a great change for the better cannot afford to miss. It contains 60 powerful positive confessions, Bible quotations, songs and prayer points that will turn your destiny around. This book is a must read if you;

* Are tired of your present situation.
* Desire positive change.
* Desire a better living condition.
* Desire Divine healing and supernatural interventions.
* Want a turnaround from the level you are in now.
* Want to discover God's purpose for your life.

As you journey through this book, you will discover God's purpose for your destiny; and if you have discovered your purpose, the book will help you to secure a better future.

THE KING'S CHAMBER PUBLICATIONS

THE KING'S CHAMBER CODE OF CONDUCT

A compilation of who a worker is, for whom he or she is working and what the work of a worker is. It is a book that spells out what the conduct of a worker should be and the rules to maintain decency in the house of God *(1Cor.14:40)*

PRAYER MANUAL VOL. 1

Is a prayer manual that contains daily prayer points for 30 days with scriptures. You can use it as guide if you are on a 30days spiritual exercise.

THE KING'S HYMNAL

Hymns invite the Spirit of the Lord, create a feeling of reverence, unify the people of God and provide a way for us to offer praises to the Lord. Some greatest sermons are preached from the singing of hymns. The King's Hymnal is a collection of hymns that can lift our souls, give us courage and move us to righteous actions. It a compilation of Hymns that fill our souls with heavenly thoughts and bring us a spirit of peace.

WHERE TO OBTAIN THESE BOOKS

THE KING'S BOOKS STORE
42, Association Avenue,
By Obanikoro Bus Stop,
Ilupeju, Lagos,
Nigeria.
Tel: 0802 963 3704, 0803 537 6075

BIBLE WONDERLAND (ALAKA-SURULERE)
Plot 33, Funsho Wiliams Avenue,
Near National Stadium,
Surulere. Lagos,

Tel: 0810 568 2169, 0810 568 2185
3. www.createspace.com
4. www.amazon.com
5. www.thekingschamberng.org
6. www.settlemeolord.org

For further help, counseling and prayers, please contact:

The King's Chamber, Headquarters
The City of Grace
42, Association Avenue,
By Obanikoro Bus Stop,
Ilupeju, Lagos, Nigeria.
Tel: 0809 985 0325, 0803 537 6075
Info@thekingschamberng.org

The King's Chamber, Ikorodu
Amazing Grace House,
216, Lagos Road,
Idi-Iroko Bus Stop, Ikorodu, Lagos.
Tel: 0803 337 0220, 0803 398 9899
kingschamberikorodu@yahoo.com

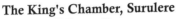

The King's Chamber, Surulere
Smile Well Event Centre,
33, Enitan Street,
Aguda, Surulere, Lagos.
Tel: 0803 320 7996, 0808 531 5225
citadeloffaith@hotmail.com

The King's Chamber, Lekki
42, Oba Yekini Elegusi Street,
By Chico Bus-StopM
Ikate, Elegusi,
Lekki
0802 307 0443, 0802 955 9522
tkc.lekki@gmail.com

If God has made this book a blessing to you and you wish to share your testimony, Reverend Afolabi Samuel Coker would love to hear from you and remember you in a moment of prayer.

Feel free to contact him on the following channels

Phone: +234 (0) 803 337 4095; +234 (0) 802 318 9259
E-mail: afocoker@yahoo.com, tutucoker@hotmail.com
Facebook: Facebook.com/afolabiandadetutucoker
Twitter: @Pastor_Coker
Blog: pastorcoker.blogspot.com

BE A PARTNER

☐ I would like to become a partner with your publication ministry

☐ I would like more copies of this particular book to be printed

☐ I would like you to print more copies of other books

NAME:

ADDRESS:

PHONE:

EMAIL:

Mailing Address: Afolabi Samuel Coker,
G. P. O. Box 7416, Akerele, Surulere,Lagos, Nigeria.